YOUR ACTING CAREER
How to Break Into and
Survive in the Theatre

Your Acting Career

HOW TO BREAK INTO AND SURVIVE IN THE THEATRE

REBECCA NAHAS

CROWN PUBLISHERS, INC., NEW YORK

Printed in the United States of America
Published simultaneously in Canada by General Publishing Company
Limited

Design: Deborah Daly

Library of Congress Cataloging in Publication Data

Nahas, Rebecca.
   Your acting career.

   Includes index.
   1. Acting as a profession. I. Title.
PN2055.N3   792'.028'023   76-3726
ISBN 0-517-52528-3
ISBN 0-517-525291 pbk

For Maryanne and Elizabeth

Acknowledgments

In writing this book I received generous assistance from Myra Turley, Maxine W. Klein, who designed the maps, Sanford I. Wolff, Burton Jacoby, Kat Brady, Linda Addeo, Amelia Haas, Albert Hall, and Tom Cuff.

For their constant encouragement and support I want to give special thanks to my Mother and Father, to George Nussrallah, to Margaret, Nancy, and Jim, and to Tony.

Contents

YOUR ACTING CAREER
How to Break Into and
Survive in the Theatre

CHAPTER 1

Starting Out:
What, Where, and How

According to the membership rolls of the professional unions, more than 20,000 actors live in New York and actively pursue their careers here. Actors Equity has 19,500 active members nationally, and a large percentage are New York-based. Equity estimates that at any given time approximately 75 percent of its members are unemployed and that, of the 25 percent employed, 80 percent earn $5,000 or less. AFTRA (American Federation of Television and Radio Artists) lists 8,700 paid-up New York members, of whom 75 percent earn $2,000 or less, 11 percent earn between $2,000 and $5,000, 7 percent earn between $5,000 and $10,000, leaving only 6 percent who earn $10,000 and above from television and commercial work. The total active membership of the New York branch of SAG (Screen Actors Guild) is 10,444. Of that number, 75 percent earn under $2,500 per year.

These figures tell you in no uncertain terms that the odds are against success for actors and actresses from the moment they arrive in New York. Everyone has heard how rough it is—that doesn't prevent thousands of new hopefuls from coming here each year. The attrition rate is high. Many leave after one year. Of those who stay, a large number end up going into another field, including jobs related to theatre—many agents, stage managers, and casting directors started out as actors.

It all boils down to this—of the thousands of actors and actresses trying to make it, only a small percentage of them do. Why? Is it luck, good timing, discovery in a drugstore, being the producer's son or the director's girl friend? While these things may have helped a few performers initially, what sustained them and made a flash-in-the-pan career into an enduring and viable one is something much less romantic and much more grueling and calculated than anyone outside the business realizes. Their secret formula is intelligent, focused, constant, hard work. Anyone can work at it: some would-be actors have for years and have never gotten anywhere. But the successful actor and actress go a step farther. They figure out *what* they have to work with, *why* and *how* they must work, *where* and *when* they must work. With everything clarified and a plan down on paper, they follow it step by step, day after day—no shortcuts. Gradually, it begins to work for them.

THE WHAT, WHY, AND HOW

Actors and actresses must find out what their acting is like. If you don't know really what you do and how well or poorly you do it, you can't begin to convince others that you're good. The first step is to gather all the information about you for you. You are not the best source. You are not the best judge of your talent. Get all the outside evaluation and helpful criticism that you can. Go to the best places and people. Go to established professionals who know the business inside out and who set themselves up as certified helpers. If you're smart, you'll go to them not just for a consultation, but you'll take advantage of their professional know-how and spend hours learning from them. What does all this mean?

The best way to find out *what* you have to work with is to go to an acting school or class and study. You're studying yourself really through the eyes of skilled professionals.

No actor gets hired because he or she shows a spark of raw talent that just needs to be refined. What director or producer has the time or money to help you or wait until you get it together?

As you meet other actors in the city, you'll find out for yourself that the ones who get jobs and are successful work at it full time. They know that they can present only themselves, but the selves they present have to be working at full creative capacity. Certainly there will be people who can outact you in an isolated situation, but the more talented person doesn't necessarily get the job.

Jobs come to the actor who is always improving and widening his range with study and self-discipline and who makes a career by constant pursuit. This is *why* you must work at acting. If you don't, no matter how talented you are, you'll get beaten out every time by the actor who worked a little harder than the rest.

So you're ready to work as hard as the next person; *how* do you do it? First of all, the next person knows what kind of acting lessons, voice lessons, and dance lessons to take in preparation.

Studying in a professional school is the most efficient means of getting a work pattern started. Schools offer a package program of acting, speech, movement, and singing classes. You get an overall picture of where you have to go in each of these areas. A variety of teachers, many of them professional performers, can guide you in improving not only your acting, but other important features—your voice, singing, and dancing.

One clarification is necessary. A *professional school* is not the same as a college or university drama department. A professional school trains applied artists who act, not theatre historians or aspiring teachers. Most universities in the United States give only a smattering of applied acting courses within an academic framework. In New York, some of the professional schools (listed later in this chapter) offer bachelor or associate degrees in theatre arts. However, these degrees represent a more concentrated and functional study of acting than does a primarily academic degree in theatre from almost any state or private college. To repeat: a degree in theatre from a school outside New York (one notable exception— Yale School of Drama) does not give proof of adequate training for an acting career in professional theatre.

Even if you have practical training in regional or community theatre or have studied under a coach or professor in your hometown or school, still give serious consideration to attending a New York professional school. Making it in New York theatre has a whole different set of rules—and, logically, New York schools have an inside line. Give yourself every kind of help available. You won't find any good school here a waste of time or money; in fact, you can be saved a lot of wasted effort if you begin your career with a solid training program in New York in the midst of the action. You must avoid shortcuts and spend adequate time in preparation.

There is one other important advantage in coming to New York to study. You will have time, before you start job-hunting and coping with the business end of acting, to get the feel of the city. If you're going to try to make it in New York, the sooner you learn about its unique challenges the better. Before you can cope with a career in the city, you have to know how to cope with the city. (More on this in a later chapter.)

Schools

The following list contains the names, addresses, and approximate costs of several reputable acting schools. Most have a full-time, two-year program. Some offer evening classes and some have an optional degree program under their own auspices or in affiliation with an outside university or college. For a full description and rundown, write for a brochure at the addresses given.

Key:
D—Degree program
E—Evening school
F—Financial aid and/or scholarships available

Stella Adler Theatre Studio
City Center, Administration Building
130 West 56th Street
New York, New York   10019
212–246–1195

2-year program; E
basic fee, $1,660 1st year
basic fee, $735 2nd year
special courses, $575

American Academy of Dramatic Arts
120 Madison Avenue
New York, New York   10016
212–686–9244

2-year program; D, E, F
total, $1,650 1st year
total, $1,250 2nd year

American Musical and Dramatic Academy
150 Bleecker Street
New York, New York   10012
212–677–5400

2-year program; D, E, F
total, $1,415 1st year
total, $1,400 2nd year

Herbert Berghof Studio
120 Bank Street
New York, New York   10014
212–OR5–2370

Classes in 19-week terms
Full time, $799 per term
Approximately $1,600 per year

Circle in the Square Theatre School
1633 Broadway
New York, New York   10019
212–581–3270

2-year program; E, F
Full time, $1,595 per year

Juilliard School
   Drama Division—Office of Admissions
   Lincoln Center
   New York, New York   10023
   212–799–5000

   4-year program; D, F
   special 2-year program for advanced students
      with degree, $2,600 per year

Neighborhood Playhouse School of the Theatre
   340 East 54th Street
   New York, New York   10022
   212–MU8–3770

   Full time, $1,700 per year

New York University
   Admissions Office
   School of the Arts
   905 Tisch Hall
   Washington Square
   New York, New York   10003
   212–598–2401

   3-year program; D, F
   total, $3,300 per year

Pratt Institute
   School of Art and Design
   Theatre Program
   Brooklyn, New York   11205
   212–636–3625

   4-year program; D, F
   $2,775 per year

When you write away for brochures, write all or many of
the schools and compare their programs. Look over carefully
how they structure their classes and see if they have a
production period (plays cast with students and performed as
part of the training). Check the list of teachers and look at
their credentials. Note schools with a heavy balance of teachers who are themselves currently performers. This indicates

an alive and aware faculty with a foothold on what is happening in theatre now.

If at all possible, come to New York for a few days or a week before you actually move here so you can visit the schools. Atmosphere and personality cannot be described in a brochure. Ask if you can audit some of the classes. Get a feel for the place and the students and faculty.

Once you decide on the school that most appeals to you, apply well before the term that you want to enter. If you have to audition for acceptance, get all the information on kinds of pieces to prepare and what they prefer—classical, modern, humorous, dramatic. If your first choice of schools does require an audition before accepting students, you should cover yourself by applying to your second, third, and fourth choices.

Prepare for your audition thoroughly; get the help of a director or professor who is known to be a good coach. Try to schedule your auditions enough ahead of when you would like to start studying so that, if you are rejected, you will have time to arrange another plan. Have alternatives in mind—other schools, perhaps, that don't require auditions for entrance—and be positive about whatever program you finally choose. Don't feel that an audition rejection means you have no talent. If you really want to act, you'll have to get used to hundreds of rejections and not let them discourage you. It takes more than one or two auditions to determine whether you should or shouldn't try to act professionally. Many of these schools will not keep students after a year of study if they judge that the person is not actor material. Don't overlook schools with this provision. They do you a favor, either by validating your talent or telling you that you are wasting your time.

Acting Teachers

If you absolutely cannot, for financial reasons or whatever, manage to take a full-time program, definitely get yourself into an acting class and follow up with singing and dance and whatever supplementary lessons you need, e.g., speech, theatre games, and so forth. You have to push yourself in all directions. Even if you never could or don't want to sing and dance, remember that they are invaluable assets to the actor. Most professional schools give their acting students at least a basic grounding in voice and movement. If you want to keep up with the competition, you would be wise to do the same.

There are hundreds of acting teachers in New York. Some are excellent, others adequate, some fraudulent. The following is a list, by no means complete or definitive, of several good acting teachers, recommended by professional theatre people.

William Esper
212–JU6–6300 (service)

Gene Feist
Roundabout Theatre Company
333 West 23rd Street
212–924–7161

Mari Gorman
The Manhattan Theatre Club
325 East 73rd Street
212–691–3237 (service)

Wynn Handman
American Place Theatre
111 West 46th Street
212–246–3730

David LeGrant
212–JU6–6300 (service)

George Morrison (Theatre Games)
212 West 29th Street
212–594–2614

Warren Robertson
1220 Broadway
212–564–1380

Michael Shurtleff
212–CH3–5689

Lee Strasberg and Associates
Lee Strasberg Theatre Institute
34 West 13th Street
212–255–2220

Before deciding on a teacher, definitely call several and ask them specific questions, such as: Do you teach beginning and/or advanced students? Do you separate them or lump everyone into the same class? Do beginners and advanced students work together or just observe one another? What goes on in class—exercises? Scene work? Other? Who teaches each class? What are the teachers' backgrounds? How long have they taught? How much do you charge? Do you expect full payment for classes before they meet? Will you allow a partial payment plan? Do you permit students to make up classes they have missed? How many times a week do you meet? How long is each class? Do you limit the number of students per class? Do you require an audition before you accept students? Do you allow would-be students to audition a second time if rejected on the first try? Do you allow private consultation on a student's progress? Is everything discussed in class before everyone? Do you have any kind of production, cast with students, worked into your program?

Finally, if you ask nothing else: May I come in and audit one of your classes before I decide to enroll? If not, why not?

As you can see, there is a lot to evaluate. Try to get as much information as possible. Compare the various teachers and their methods. Auditing—observing how a class is conducted, what the students do, how the teachers work with them, deciding if you can see yourself learning from that kind of instruction—is an invaluable help in deciding on a teacher.

Specialty Teachers—How to Find Them

A list of specialty teachers in singing, dance, stage movement, speech, and the like would in itself fill a book. There are several ways of finding them.

Many teachers advertise in the trade papers such as *Back-*

stage or *Show Business* (hereafter referred to as "the trades"), weeklies published especially for actors, available at newsstands for fifty cents. Both contain virtually the same casting calls, announcements, and advertising. Check in the *Village Voice*, a weekly newspaper, and *Dance* magazine for leads on various dance and movement teachers.

You might try calling one of the professional schools listed earlier in this chapter for the names of their teachers who conduct outside classes, or ask them to recommend someone to you.

You can check the bulletin boards at Actors Equity for leads on teachers. Equity is located at 1500 Broadway on the fourth floor. Although the lounge for actors has a sign saying "Union Members Only," you can ignore it. Just walk in as if you know what you're doing and go up to the bulletin boards, which list a variety of things—auditions, play announcements, classes, and so forth.

Another good bulletin board is located at Drama Book Shop at 150 West 52nd Street. You should become acquainted with this store anyway. It has the largest selection of published plays in the city, and the people behind the counter are very helpful.

One of the best ways of finding out about good specialty teachers is to ask other actors or acting students for their recommendations. If you see a good performance, go backstage and ask that actor where he or she studies.

Ask advice often, scan the papers and bulletin boards, and, before enrolling, see if you can audit a class—this is a common practice. Don't ever hesitate to pull out of any class or private lesson that is not—after an adequate period of time—helping you. Every singing and dance teacher has his or her own style and personality; these can be either conducive or detrimental to your progress. Find the teacher who suits you.

How to Avoid Quacks

The best protection against quacks is to check out, with someone in the know, any teacher you find through an advertisement or by recommendation.

Generally, you should try to find others who have studied

under, or at least heard of, a teacher you find through an advertisement. Do not go to any private home for a lesson without first checking on the reputability of the teacher. You could try calling the paper where you found the ad and asking if they have checked out the teacher's credits. Sometimes, not always, the trades act responsibly about their advertisers. However, they cannot check out everyone.

You can call one of the unions for actors—Equity is a good start (869–8530)—and ask if they know anything about the person.

If you can't find anyone among your actor and student friends who has heard of this teacher or, better yet, someone who studies with him or her, forget it and keep looking. Good teachers have followings. Why risk wasting your time with an unknown?

How Much Do Lessons Cost?

The costs of professional schools and those that offer scholarship-aid programs have been noted earlier in the chapter. Individual acting classes cost anywhere from $40 to $80 per month.

As for dance classes, you can expect to pay from $3 to $4.50 per lesson or $25 to $40 for a ten-lesson card. Many dance studios give a further discount to union members.

Most singing teachers charge on a per-lesson basis, as do singing coaches. The difference, by the way, is that a coach works with you on songs and professional audition techniques. A singing teacher usually concentrates on vocal exercises and overall voice development. (Some teachers do both.) Voice lessons cost $10 to $30 for a 30-to-60-minute session.

You can find instructors for everything. You may want someone to help you with a specific audition preparation or a particular speech problem (regionalisms, for example). Always follow the quack-prevention code—check out everyone beforehand and ask ahead of time what the teacher charges. Do some comparison shopping and make sure you know what is the approximate going rate. Shop around until you find the right teacher with the right price.

What Goes On in Classes?

Singing, dance, speech classes follow similar patterns. Each teacher usually has a series of exercises that begin each class. What happens after that varies somewhat. Some singing lessons (usually lasting from one-half hour to an hour at the most) will be all vocal exercises. Some teachers will spend time working on songs. Either you or the teacher will choose a song that you probably will work on in a technical way—phrase by phrase—almost as if the song were an exercise with words. Remember, singing teachers differ from coaches in this respect. The emphasis with a teacher (the semantics may vary) is on vocal quality and range and the technical aspects of your singing. For specific song work, you probably will have to go to a coach. If you have never studied voice, you should go first to a teacher, and when he or she feels you're ready for song work, then you can look for a coach. Your teacher will be able to recommend someone.

Eventually, if you want to go to singing auditions, you'll learn first what kind of singer you are—soprano, mezzo soprano, tenor, alto, bass—and your range. You'll learn the difference between a "legit" voice and a "belt." You'll learn the different styles of songs that you will need in your repetoire, to prepare you for every kind of singing audition. For example, you may be asked to come with a ballad and an up-tune. Your teacher will be able to fill you in on all this. We'll talk about actual singing auditions in a later chapter.

Dance lessons—ballet, jazz, tap—last at least an hour, sometimes two, usually an hour and a half. Like singing lessons, they all begin with the teacher's own exercise routine. Many of you have been to dance classes and know what to expect. For those of you who have never studied dance, most professional teachers recommend that you take ballet first. Ballet gives a basic technique and conditioning important to all forms of dance.

The exercises, warm-ups, stretches, are followed usually by isolated practice on technique—pirouettes, turns, spotting—and/or working on a routine. The teacher creates a "combination" that he or she demonstrates and then teaches the students. Usually, you work on this for the remainder of the class.

What goes on in acting class is not easily predictable. Every acting teacher has his own method and, as you would expect, beginning classes can vary enormously from more advanced ones. As a rule, no generalizations are possible—a teacher may have the equivalent of warm-up exercises for his beginning students: sense-memory exercises, "as if" exercises, object exercises, rhythm exercises, and improvisations are some of the better known. These may be done both individually and in groups.

At some point, you will graduate into scene work—or you may begin at this level. The teacher assigns you and one or two other students a scene; monologue work is not done so frequently. Usually, you will have a few days to prepare and then you'll bring it in and perform it for the class. The teacher and/or students then comment and constructively criticize, and you will work over the scene once, probably many times, more.

The teacher may have you choose your own scenes and partners. The choice of working or not each week or each class may be left up to you also. If possible, make yourself prepare and get up and do a scene for every class. You can learn something from just observing, but much more if you work each class. You'll find there is less anxiety about getting up in front of others if you do so regularly rather than sporadically.

Acting classes can last from one to four hours a session, sometimes more. Obviously, a smaller class is better for the student because more individual attention is permitted. A good teacher will see to it that the size of his class is limited.

How Long Do You Study?

If you're not enrolled in an acting school designed to monitor individual progress and turn out professionals within a certain time limit, how will you know when you're ready?

You can continue taking classes throughout your pro-

fessional career, but at some point you must begin auditioning for shows. When? To a certain extent, you can become
your own judge. You'll be able to discern your progress in
acting class under the guidance of a good teacher, and you'll
learn about your own work by observing other actors and
how they improve from class to class.

When you reach a certain level of skill, your acting needs a
testing ground. Professional schools have periods of performance or productions built into their curricula. Students
are cast in various plays in roles suited to their level. If you
are taking acting classes only, or different kinds of classes in
different places and your acting coach doesn't have any
productions included in his method of teaching, then, eventually, you should try to get into a play.

The first auditioning you do, when you and your teacher
decide you're ready, doesn't have to be for a "professional"
show. In fact, it is probably better if you look into the
various showcase productions in the city. A showcase can be
a valuable halfway house for beginning actors. This allows
you to work, usually under professional conditions but for
no pay, with rehearsals adjusted to the company's outside
commitments, for a limited number of performances. This is
usually what "Off-Off Broadway" means.

Officially, according to Actors Equity, a showcase is de-
fined as "a non-profit production participated in by Equity
Members [almost all showcases audition and use non-Equity
actors as well] for the purpose of presenting scenes and/or a
play for the benefit of the participating Actors in limited
semi-public performance where *no obligatory* admission fee
in any form is paid." Showcase Theatres may accept con-
tributions or donations at the door and seating capacity
cannot exceed one hundred. The showcase code is now under
study by Equity and some changes may be forthcoming.

Many showcase theatres, not all, follow Equity's guidelines. Almost every one does audition and use non-Equity
performers, which is good for you since you probably won't
have union affiliation at this beginning stage of your career.

The audition announcements for showcases, listing play,
cast rundown, location of theatre, and time of audition and
interview, are carried in the trades or posted on bulletin

boards. Begin buying *Backstage* and/or *Show Business*—they reach most newsstands every Thursday—and check all the showcase auditions. Decide on the ones that most appeal to you, make sure they will audition non-Equity actors, and give them a try.

Usually, it is better to go toward the beginning of the call time. Showcase auditions get large turnouts and the wait can be long and annoying. If you like, look over the play ahead of time (if it is published) and study the character or characters closest to your type. When you arrive and sign the list, you may be given a copy of the play or a side (section of the script) to read and prepare. If they don't indicate which scene you'll be doing—ask. Give whatever preparation time you wish to the script and then wait for your turn. The best way to find out how to prepare yourself for an audition, showcase or otherwise, is by going to several, trying different methods, and settling on what is right for you. Every actor has a different approach. Some like to seclude themselves, read the scene over many times, even memorize it if possible. Others prefer giving a cold reading with very little preparation. Some actors do physical and vocal warm-ups and some just kibitz with the crowd. Most actors will agree that they give their best reading when they go in with a positive, relaxed attitude. If you are nervous at auditions—who isn't?—work at conquering the jitters or find a way to rise above them or to use the energy they stir up in a positive way.

Auditions for showcases are themselves very helpful. You can learn a great deal about your acting and the areas you need to work on. Consider these auditions as tools, as means of analyzing and improving your work. You may want to take a scene from an audition to your acting class and find out what you did right or wrong. Don't let showcase auditions frighten or depress you. Even though you may not be cast or feel as if you were a smash, you can use every one for your own growth. Good acting comes from finding out what you do wrong and eliminating it.

Here are the names of some showcase theatres in New York. For a complete list contact the Off-Off Broadway Alliance, 245 West 52nd Street, New York, New York 10019 (212—757—4473).

Actors' Experimental Unit, Inc.
682 Avenue of the Americas
New York, New York   10010

Amas Repertory Theatre, Inc.
Church of St. Paul and St. Andrew
263 West 86th Street
New York, New York   10024

Central Arts
108 East 64th Street
New York, New York   10021

CSC Repertory
Abbey Theatre
136 East 13th Street
New York, New York   10003

The Cubiculo
414 West 51st Street
New York, New York   10019

Drama Tree Players
182 Fifth Avenue
New York, New York   10010

Dramatis Personae, Inc.
114 West 14th Street
New York, New York   10011

Interart Theatre
Women's Interart Center
549 West 52nd Street
New York, New York   10019

INTAR (International Arts Relations, Inc.)
508 West 53rd Street
New York, New York   10019

The Jean Cocteau Repertory, Bouwerie Lane Theatre
330 Bowery
New York, New York   10012

Manhattan Project Theatre Company
  c/o New York University School of the Arts
  111 Second Avenue
  New York, New York   10003

Manhattan Theatre Club, Inc.
  321 East 73rd Street
  New York, New York   10021

New York Theatre Ensemble
  62 East 4th Street
  New York, New York   10003

The Performance Group
  33 Wooster Street
  New York, New York   10003

Shaliko
  New York University School of the Arts
  40 East 7th Street
  New York, New York   10003

South Street Theatre
  16 Fulton Street
  New York, New York   10038

Theatre at St. Clement's
  423 West 46th Street
  New York, New York   10036

Theatre for the New City
  113 Jane Street
  New York, New York   10014

Urban Arts Corps, Inc.
  26 West 20th Street
  New York, New York   10011

When you begin auditioning for showcases, consider yourself entering a new phase. Everything you were doing before as a student may continue and you may not discern any difference in your acting or your attitude. But the showcases represent a kind of rite of passage. They are an initiation into the world of acting. The routine you establish in searching out, auditioning for, and being in showcases is the groundwork for your later job-hunting. You can afford to make all your mistakes in this period without losing anything. You have only to gain a wealth of learning experience and subsequent growth.

This phase is as invaluable as your formal training. Schools set you on the right track and give you some essential guidelines about acting, but the bulk of your learning will come, and has to, from what you do on stage, in rehearsal and performance.

Don't sell showcases short. You'll discover that professional actors, well established in the business, frequently audition for and do showcases. Exposure to their work is another benefit for the beginning actor. Frequently, the quality of the script and the acting in a showcase equal and may surpass anything on or off Broadway. On occasion, showcases may be so well received that a producer will come along and finance the show for full production. (The original actors may be used, but are sometimes *replaced with compensation.* Equity's rules are very specific on this.)

There is no set time limit to your showcase phase; actors feel differently about how much showcase work they need or want. Some actors spend two or three years doing nothing but showcases—by choice. Others audition for them because they can't find any paying jobs and they want to act. Some actors reach a saturation point and refuse to do any more showcases. You will have to be your own judge. You don't want to make a lifetime out of showcases, but they can be a helpful transition from study to regular job-hunting and paying work.

Don't pay attention to any talk of "nothing can happen until you get your Equity card." It is true that you must be a member to audition for most Broadway and Off-Broadway shows, but having a card is no guarantee of work. It means you have to pay dues and be careful to avoid any non-Equity productions. You can easily afford to hold off getting a card until you feel you are ready to work at working professionally, full time. (How to get a card will be discussed later.)

Finally, there is one important point to make. The type of training and preparation described in this chapter—geared toward stage work—is vital to all actors and actresses, whether they intend to work on the legitimate stage or in television, films, or commercials.

Without a solid grounding in legitimate theatre, very few actors and actresses can break into films and television or get any advertising agency to consider them for commercials. When casting directors for films, TV, or commercials look at your résumé, they want to see stage credits—the more the better. Broadway, Off-Broadway, touring, stock, regional, dinner theatre—even some showcase work—label you as an experienced, serious performer who will bring class and a broad acting range to any film, TV show, or commercial.

With a solid theatre background, when and if you decide to try to get work in any of these other areas, you can acquire the particular skills they demand. Of course, there are special classes that can help you: "How to Make Commercials," soap opera workshops, and so forth. More on these in a later chapter.   •

Meanwhile, give all your energies to getting the basics down: train as a stage actor first. Challenge yourself constantly and don't be afraid to make mistakes and fall on your face. That's what learning to act is about. Exploration and discovery. Trying every approach and emotion and finding the right ones.

Has anything been overlooked? What about those two old specters, motivation and talent? It seems ridiculous to belabor the fact that without a lot of the former and at least a modicum of the latter you shouldn't try to act professionally. Do you have enough motivation and talent to make it? If you think so, then go ahead and try. The worst that can happen is that you'll discover you were wrong and you'll want to quit. But at least you won't spend the rest of your life wondering if you cheated yourself out of an acting career. Chances are you will have enough talent and motivation to see you through. It is not such a rare combination, and sometimes a heavy dose of one can make up for a lack of the other. But neither of them can substitute for "intelligent, focused, constant hard work." That's the backbone of any successful acting career.

CHAPTER 2

Surviving in New York

There is more to living in New York than just going about your business the way a normal person does in any other city. If you want to survive and move with the crowds, you have to become city-wise.

You can't possibly absorb everything: the people who approach you for money, the crazies who talk incoherently or stand screaming at passersby, the buildings, the food. You can't take it all in, so you define the limits of your private world inside the vastness of New York and try to deal sanely with the rest of it.

You numb yourself to the environment; you're wise to the place and aloof. You begin to spot tourists and feel superior to them. You walk quickly down the streets, full of the importance of your destination. You cross on a red light, you take your place in the pedestrian showdown with buses and cars and taxis. You get a bit arrogant, a bit pushy, and you watch out for yourself. This is part of the New York survival kit.

I remember once entertaining a friend from a small town in Pennsylvania. We were on a subway one afternoon and a young boy walked through the car with a tin cup and a cane. My friend, moved with compassion to help out the blind boy, put a ten-dollar bill in the cup and then whispered to the boy the denomination of the bill so he would know what he had. When the youth streaked off the train at the next stop, I felt my admonition to my friend was justified. Didn't he know the boy was just a hustler? Well, I knew or thought I did. That's city-wise.

WHERE TO LIVE?

If you know before coming to New York where you'll be studying, you may be able to arrange ahead of time for housing. If you can tolerate dormitory living for a year or a few months, your expenses will be kept low and you won't have to worry immediately about setting up house.

Of the professional schools listed, only New York University and Pratt Institute provide dormitory facilities. (See individual brochures.)

The American Academy, which offers an optional co-ordinated program with Pace College in Manhattan, suggests the Pace University Residence Towers. See the Academy's brochure for more information.

The Juilliard School's Information Office will provide a list of staff-approved living accommodations in the vicinity. See the Juilliard catalog.

Men's and Women's Residences

Another alternative to apartment living is a residence house or hotel. Many pleasant, relatively inexpensive places exist, ranging from YMCAs and YWCAs to the more elaborate, for girls, Barbizon Hotel for Women. Besides a better price, these places usually offer greater security and a more personalized environment than a regular hotel.

The following list contains the names, addresses, phone numbers, and present rental fees of some of the residential

hotels in New York. Keep in mind that many of these places
have long waiting lists and should be booked well in advance
of your arrival date.

For Men and Women

International House, 500 Riverside Drive, 212–678–5000.
$37 weekly, $95–$128 (students only).

Pennington, 215 East 15th Street, 212–GR5–9193. $10
nightly, $48 weekly (2 meals included).

Phoebe Warren Residence, 8 East 68th Street, 212–RE7–
1073. $45–$50 weekly.

Retreat House, 434 West 20th Street, 212–924–9517.
$155–$180 monthly.

West Side YMCA, 5 West 63rd Street, 212–787–4400.
$9.75 nightly, $39 weekly.

William Sloane House, 356 West 34th Street, 212–
695–5000. $9 nightly (1st 2 weeks) $38.50 weekly.

For Men

Grand Central YMCA, 224 East 47th Street, 212–755–
2410. $8.50–$9 nightly (weekly rate worked out after 2
week period of residence).

McBurney YMCA, 215 West 23rd Street, 212–243–1982.
$6.75–$7.25 nightly, $31–$33.75 weekly.

For Women

Allerton House for Women, 130 East 57th Street, 212–
753–8841. $10–$12–$14 nightly, $46–$73 weekly.

Barbizon Hotel for Women Lexington and 63rd Street,
212–TE8–5700. $48–$77 weekly.

Brandon House, 340 West 85th Street, 212–787–1212.
$37.50 weekly (2 meals included).

Evangeline, 123 West 13th Street, 212–242–2400. $50
weekly (2 meals).

Ladies Christian Union of the City of New York, 118 West
13th Street. All branches about $45 weekly (2 meals).

Katherine House
118 West 13th Street
212–242–6566

Millbank Memorial House
11 West 10th Street
212–475–9720

Roberts House
151 East 36th Street
212–683–6865

Sage House
49 West 9th Street
212–473–1256

Martha Washington, 29 East 29th Street, 212–689–1900. $42–$56 weekly.

Parkside Evangeline, 18 Gramercy Park South, 212–677–6200. $51.80–$54.80 weekly (2 meals).

Rehearsal Club, 47 West 53rd Street, 212–CO5–9207. $50 weekly (2 meals), especially for women in the arts; must audition for acceptance; long waiting list.

St. Mary's Residence, 225 East 72nd Street, 212–249–6850. $50 weekly.

St. Zita's, 141 West 14th Street, 212–CH3–7200. Dormitory (4 to a room) $18 weekly, single $30 weekly.

Simmons House, 350 West 88th Street, 212–724–6100. $33–$52 weekly.

Swiss Town House, 35 West 67th Street, 212–787–1130. Double $44 (2 meals), single $50.

YWCA Residence, 135 East 52nd Street, 212–PL3–4700. $9–$9.50 per day (2 week maximum stay).

Young Women's Towne House, 53 East 43rd Street (top of Hotel Biltmore), 212–490–0345. $8–$10–$12 nightly.

Apartment Living

If you choose to begin apartment living as soon as you arrive in New York, you have more work cut out for you.

Unless you have friends already settled here whose apartment you are going to share or who know of an apartment that will be available for you, plan on at least a month of searching. You may be lucky and locate an ideal place in your first week in the city, but you can't depend on luck.

This means arranging for temporary housing before you arrive. You might choose one of the residences just listed or plan to move in with a friend. Be sure you and your friend discuss this realistically ahead of time. Can he or she, even temporarily, stand another body around—space-wise and head-wise? What will the financial arrangement be—sharing rent, food, telephone, electric and gas bills? Whatever arrangement you reach, make sure your friend and his or her roommates and you discuss it thoroughly. Better to anticipate trouble and avoid it than be stuck in an unpleasant situation.

Decide if your temporary residence can handle all your belongings. You may want to bring only the essentials and ship out the rest when you have your own place. If you know when your classes begin, try to come ahead of time, ideally a month or two, at least a week, to start the search for an apartment.

Before you even begin to look, answer a few basic questions. How much *rent* can you afford to pay? The answer to this will influence the second question: What *size* apartment do you want? Presumably, we'd all love a ten-room penthouse, but often our budget can tolerate only a studio (single room apartment). Both these previous questions may influence the last two: Do you want a *roommate?* What *location* do you want?

Juggle around these four questions: price? size? roommates? location? and come up with the ideal apartment setup for you. If you can afford a studio, don't mind a single room, want to live alone, and know you want to be in midtown, you can begin looking with that specific arrangement in mind. Knowing exactly what you want makes looking a lot easier. Also, decide—according to how long you can wait to find the right place—if you are willing to compromise. Time and money limitations may demand flexibility.

Price

The following is a table of apartment prices on today's market. You'll notice the list is broken down into size, furnished, and unfurnished.

Size	Furnished	Unfurnished
1, 1½ rooms (studio with or without kitchenette)	$135–$330 Low High	$110–$225 Low High
2, 2½ rooms (separate bedroom)	$200–$400 Low High	$175–$350 Low High
3, 4, 5 rooms	$250–$550 Low High	$225–$500 Low High

(These figures represent *monthly* rental fees. Lower prices usually indicate less desirable quality and location.)

Prices change so rapidly in New York that this list may be outdated at your reading. Chances are that prices won't be less in the future, so you have an idea of the least you can expect to pay in rentals.

Size and Condition

When deciding on the size of your apartment, remember that you need enough space for comfort, storage, and privacy (if you plan to have roommates.)

A studio apartment or efficiency for one person can be adequate if it is well laid out. If it is one room, you'll want it as large as possible, but, besides actual footage, look for adequate closet space and workable kitchen and bath facilities. Check out the plumbing; flush the toilet once or twice, run the shower or bath. Are the refrigerator and stove in good working order? Is there any counter and cabinet space? Consider the lighting; if you have only one room, you may want as much sun as possible. Think carefully about how you can utilize the space and make the studio a comfortable home.

Run the same tests on larger apartments: check out the plumbing and kitchen facilities and the closet space. Decide if you and your rommates, if any, can afford the money and time to furnish an apartment. If not, don't waste energy looking at unfurnished listings.

Do make sure that any furnished apartment has the bare essentials (you can supplement and usually put unwanted furniture in the building basement). Check the beds for bedbugs. Look for a fresh paint job (or secure the promise of one from the landlord), workable windows, enough electrical outlets, and a minimum of roaches. (Face it, roaches abound in New York in every section but they can be controlled, and a conscientious landlord who has an exterminator come in regularly is a big help.) Check out the entryway and halls for cleanliness and good lighting; make sure there are free janitor and repair services, locked, sturdy mailboxes, and a way to dispose of garbage.

If you expect to have roommates, you'll need an apartment that can offer some measure of privacy. This may mean separate bedrooms or a room where you or your roommate can choose to retreat if the other has in friends, if you want to prepare for some class, or if you just need to be alone for a while.

Security

Security, i.e., burglary- and intruder-prevention and fire-escape precautions, is an important consideration.

An apartment building must have a locked main entrance. A doorman and/or elevator operator is desirable. But many apartment buildings in New York (especially small brownstones—converted two-family homes—usually walk-ups) do not have them. If there is no doorman, the building should at least have a working intercom system that allows you to find out who is ringing your bell before you buzz anyone in.

Is the door to the roof secured against easy entry? Since the roof is often the way in and out for burglars, the top-floor apartment can be especially prone to break-ins. Make sure the door to the apartment has a heavy frame, preferably steel, and a good lock or two. (You can always put in your own lock; more on locks later in this chapter.)

If the apartment is on ground or street level or accessible from the roof, the windows should have bars. Burglary is a fact of life for every apartment dweller. Not everyone is a victim. You don't have to be. You can lessen your vulnerability by demanding these basic precautions in the apartment building you choose.

Notice if there is a fire escape or second stairway. Ask if the building has a sprinkler system or fire-retarding walls. Be sure the cellar or basement is free of inflammable materials.

Roommates

Whether to have a roommate or not involves more than financial considerations. If you have never lived away from home and have no experience with roommate living, consider the following. Do you like having someone around? Are you share-oriented? How important is privacy to you? Are you willing to compromise? Answer these questions truthfully for yourself. Shared living is just that—a lot of sharing.

If you decide you want a roommate, be discriminating. If you are thinking of a good friend, realistically appraise your full-time compatibility. Sometimes it is easier having a stranger for a roommate. You can both go about your business and not have to deal with each other as intimately as with a good friend.

To a certain extent, you can control the degree of shared living. If you have a large enough apartment, you can manage desired privacy quite easily. In certain situations, you may not even have to see your roommate for days. If this appeals to you, consider for roommates airline stewardesses or people with traveling jobs.

Look for a roommate who understands and tolerates the life-style of actors. You may have to rehearse or prepare for a class at home. You may keep strange hours when working at an acting or a supplementary part-time job. Your income may be erratic. Your roommate must be prepared to accept you and your commitment to acting.

Is it best to have another actor as a roommate? Not necessarily. In this situation, you may find yourself drawn into competition, even if you and your roommate are only students. Acting is a very competitive profession; with actors as roommates, you may be extending your outside career into your home.

On the other hand, an actor-roommate can be a comfort and a help during your period of study and later when you turn professional. Judge if you have the capacity and desire to live in a constructive relationship with an actor as a roommate.

If you choose to live with friends, you won't have to bother looking through ads. If you want someone in theatre, go to the bulletin boards at your school, at the actors' unions (AFTRA, Equity, SAG), at Drama Book Shop, at the places actors frequent.

You can always check out the bulletin boards in college bookstores such as the Book Forum and Columbia University Bookstore, both on or near Columbia University campus at 116th Street and Broadway; the Eighth Street Bookstore at Eighth Street between Fifth Avenue and Avenue of the Americas, and nearby New York University Bookstore on Washington Place, or New York University's Loeb Student Union at LaGuardia Place and West Fourth Street.

You may want to go to a roommate service. Expect to prepay a $35 fee for a two-month contract. The advantage is that these services have immediate access to a variety of roommate possibilities and probably will offer you several choices.

Here are the names of two roommate services:

> Mamselle in Manhattan
> 141 East 55th Street
> 212–755–8817

> Two for the Money
> 415 Lexington Avenue
> 212–687–0600

No matter if you find a potential roommate through friends or bulletin boards, a newspaper or roommate service, definitely meet with the person before you make any plans. Find out as much about the person and his or her habits as possible. This is someone you may have to see every day and trust with your home and belongings and, importantly, a person you want to be able to relax with and enjoy. Be discriminating.

Location

Deciding where to live in New York hinges on three basic issues: convenience, safety, and finances. New York is divided into five boroughs: Brooklyn, the Bronx, Manhattan, Queens, and Staten Island. The majority of theatres and training schools and specialized teachers are located in Manhattan. Of the other boroughs, Brooklyn is the most agreeable for commuting, with the Bronx lagging behind in third place. Living in Queens or Staten Island would be a strain for any actor who has to be in Manhattan regularly and doesn't want to spend an hour or so getting there.

While Manhattan may be a little more expensive than Brooklyn or the Bronx, it is certainly the most convenient borough of New York for actors. You will use it more than any of the others; you will have to know how to get around in it; you should try to live in it at least until you make it your friend.

Manhattan divides into several distinct sections. Most people choose an area that best fits their life-style and their pocket. Since most areas are near a bus or subway line, getting to work or school in another section is not difficult. Of course, the cheapest means of transportation is walking, and your budget will be happier if you can find an apartment near where you'll be studying, unless your school is in a high-income neighborhood or you are not a full-time student taking all your classes in one place.

Once you turn professional and begin job-hunting, you will find yourself all over Manhattan, so no one section will be that much more convenient than another. Then again, if you land a steady job on a soap opera (the closest an actor comes to a nine-to-five existence), you might want to choose an apartment near your studio. However, no acting job ever comes with a lifetime guarantee. The majority of them are relatively short-lived and may take you hundreds of miles from your home base.

The following maps should help you visualize the layout of Manhattan. Notice that the first one delineates the various sections of the city, while the second is a street and avenue guide. (You may want to cut out these maps and keep them in your purse or wallet. Manhattan is not a difficult city to navigate, and, with a map, you can easily get yourself pointed in the right direction.)

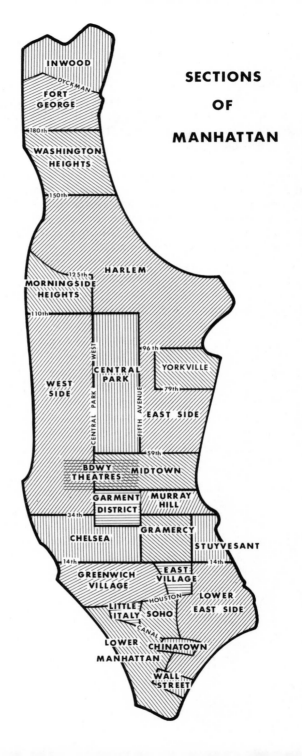

SECTIONS

OF

MANHATTAN

INWOOD

DYCKMAN

FORT GEORGE

180th

WASHINGTON HEIGHTS

150th

HARLEM

125th

MORNINGSIDE HEIGHTS

110th

CENTRAL PARK WEST

CENTRAL PARK

FIFTH AVENUE

96th

YORKVILLE

79th

WEST SIDE

EAST SIDE

59th

BDWY THEATRES

MIDTOWN

GARMENT DISTRICT

MURRAY HILL

34th

CHELSEA

GRAMERCY

STUYVESANT

14th

14th

GREENWICH VILLAGE

EAST VILLAGE

LOWER EAST SIDE

HOUSTON

LITTLE ITALY

SOHO

CANAL

LOWER MANHATTAN

CHINATOWN

WALL STREET

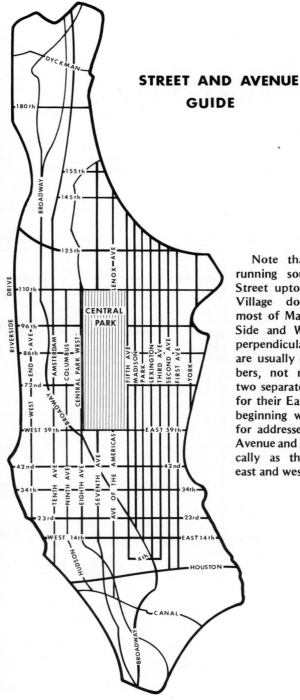

STREET AND AVENUE GUIDE

Note that Fifth Avenue, running south from 145th Street uptown to Greenwich Village downtown, divides most of Manhattan into East Side and West Side. Blocks perpendicular to Fifth Avenue are usually designed by numbers, not names, and have two separate sets of addresses for their East and West sides, beginning with low numbers for addresses closest to Fifth Avenue and increasing numerically as the streets extend east and west.

The Broadway theatre district concentrates on the West Side in the Forties and Fifties. This map designates the major houses.

BROADWAY THEATRES

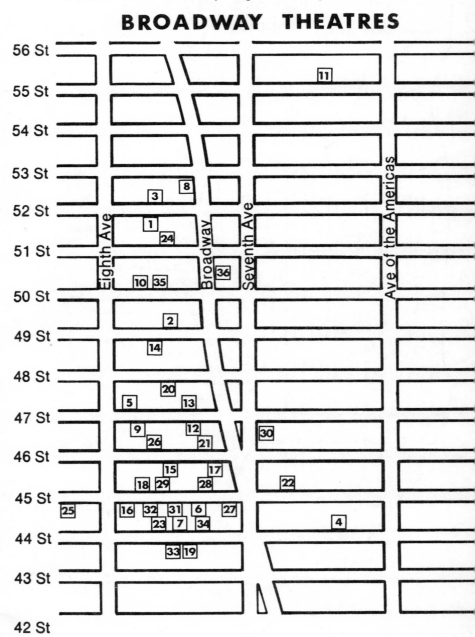

1.	Alvin	250 West 52nd Street	757-8646
2.	Ambassador	215 West 49th Street	265-1855
3.	ANTA	245 West 52nd Street	246-6270
4.	Belasco	111 West 44th Street	586-7950
5.	Biltmore	261 West 47th Street	582-5340
6.	Booth	222 West 45th Street	246-5969
7.	Broadhurst	235 West 44th Street	246-6699
8.	Broadway	1681 Broadway (53rd Street)	247-7992
9.	Brooks Atkinson	256 West 47th Street	245-3430
10.	Circle in the Square	1633 Broadway (50th Street)	581-0720
11.	City Center	131 West 55th Street	246-8989
12.	Edison	240 West 47th Street	757-7164
13.	Ethel Barrymore	243 West 47th Street	246-0390
14.	Eugene O'Neill	230 West 49th Street	246-0220
15.	Forty-Sixth Street	226 West 46th Street	246-4271
16.	Golden	252 West 45th Street	246-6740
17.	Helen Hayes	210 West 46th Street	246-6380
18.	Imperial	249 West 45th Street	265-2412
19.	Little Theatre	244 West 44th Street	221-3677
20.	Longacre	220 West 48th Street	246-5639
21.	Lunt-Fontanne	205 West 46th Street	586-5555
22.	Lyceum	149 West 45th Street	582-3897
23.	Majestic	245 West 44th Street	246-0730
24.	Mark Hellinger	237 West 51st Street	757-7064
25.	Martin Beck	302 West 45th Street	246-6363
26.	Mayfair	235 West 46th Street	221-8191
27.	Minskoff	45th Street & Broadway	869-0550
28.	Morosco	217 West 45th Street	246-6230
29.	Music Box	239 West 45th Street	246-4636
30.	Palace	1564 Broadway (47th Street)	757-2626
31.	Plymouth	236 West 45th Street	246-9156
32.	Royale	242 West 45th Street	245-5760
33.	St. James	246 West 44th Street	695-5858
34.	Shubert	225 West 44th Street	246-5990
35.	Uris	1633 Broadway (51st Street)	586-6510
36.	Winter Garden	1634 Broadway (50th Street)	245-4878
off Map			
	Billy Rose	208 West 41st Street	947-5510
	Vivian Beaumont	Lincoln Center, Broadway & 66th Street	362-7616

Many, not all, Off-Broadway theatres are located in Greenwich Village. Here is a map of the Village theatre district. (Other Off-Broadway houses, about fifteen, are scattered around Manhattan. One or two are in Brooklyn. See list on the following page for names and addresses.)

OFF BROADWAY THEATRES
GREENWICH VILLAGE

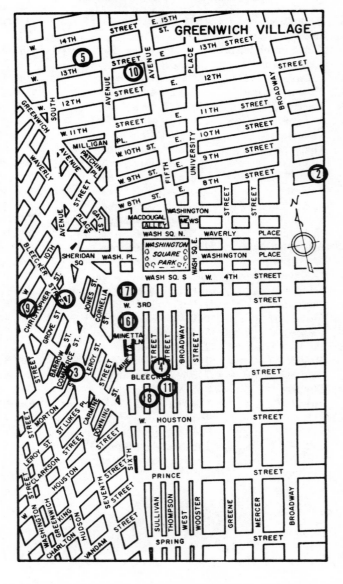

1.	Actors Playhouse	100 Seventh Avenue South	242-9657
2.	Astor Place Theatre	434 Lafayette Street	254-4370
3.	Cherry Lane Theatre	38 Commerce Street	989-2020
4.	Circle in the Square Theatre	159 Bleecker Street	254-6330
5.	Greenwich Mews Theatre	141 West 13th Street	243-6800
6.	Players Theatre	115 MacDougal	254-5076
7.	Provincetown Playhouse	133 MacDougal	730-9463
8.	Sullivan Street Playhouse	181 Sullivan Street	674-3838
9.	Theatre De Lys	121 Christopher Street	924-8782
10.	Thirteenth Street Theatre	50 West 13th Street	924-9785
11.	Village Gate	160 Bleecker Street	473-7270
	Top of the Gate	160 Bleecker Street	982-9292

Map reprinted by permission of *The Village Voice*.
Copyright © The Village Voice, Inc., 1975.

NOT ON MAP

American Place Theatre, 111 West 46th Street; 247–0393
Chelsea Theatre, Brooklyn Academy of Music, 30 Lafayette
   Avenue, Brooklyn; 636–4100
Circle Repertory Co., 99 Seventh Avenue South; 924–7100
Eastside Playhouse, 334 East 74th Street; 861–2287
Equity Library Theatre, Riverside Drive and 103rd Street;
663–2880
Jan Hus, 351 East 74th Street; 288–6743
Martinique, Broadway and 32nd Street; 736–7341
Promenade, 2162 Broadway; 799–7690
Public Theatre, 425 Lafayette Street; 677–6350
Roundabout, 333 West 23rd Street; 924–7161
Stage 73, 321 East 73rd Street; 288–2500
Theatre Four, 424 West 55th Street; 246–8545
Westside Theatre, 407 West 43rd Street; 541–8394

Television, commercial, and film auditioning and work can
take you all over the midtown section from east to west, with
an occasional foray into the Village or Upper East Side (there
is one television studio in Brooklyn).

Apartment rentals in the different neighborhoods of Manhattan vary—sometimes outrageously. The East Side, from just above the Village to the low Nineties, is generally more expensive than the West Side. Overall, the West Side—uptown, midtown, and upper downtown (the East Village is cheaper than the West Village), offers more reasonable rentals. However, each section contains exceptions; certain blocks or buildings on both sides of town can either be an isolated bargain or high-priced aberration.

Your best guides on pricing the different neighborhoods are the newspapers' real estate sections, a helpful realty office, other New Yorkers, and your own common sense. Find out which sections fit into your budget and make a few field trips. Walk around and get the feel of the different areas. Look for markets, drugstores, laundromats, convenient transit lines, and other essentials that fit your needs and your pocket. You'll discover that each section has a distinct flavor and mix. Find the ones that appeal to you and confine your apartment hunt to them.

Safety is an impotant consideration in choosing a location. Generally, you can assume that cheap, cheap rental areas such as the Lower East Side or East Harlem approach the unsavory rather than the genteel. However, no section is crime-free or freak-free. The number of winos may be greater on the Lower East Side, but even the most luxurious blocks such as Sutton Place in the east Fifties have their share of burglaries, muggings, and misdemeanors.

On your field trips (during the day, please), your eyes will tell you if the area's regular street people are not your type. Remember, however, that what you see is not an immediate threat to your person. It is just what you have to put up with on a day-to-day basis. You'll never find a crime-free area, but you can search out the blocks—there are some in every neighborhood—that have respectful and caring inhabitants. Block associations in New York have gone a long way in cleaning up and making safer (with sodium street lights and private block guards) previously troubled areas. If you like a block or section on the outside, but aren't sure of its safety, call either the Federation of West Side Block Associations (663–7766) or the East Side equivalent and find out if the area you like has a block association. Get the name of one of the officers and call for a security check on the block. Then trust your instincts and prepare to assimilate. No matter which section you choose, always take your own precautions at home, on the block, on the streets. (Specifics on safety later in this chapter.)

After you make informed decisions on your *price* range, desired *size* and *condition* requirements, whether or not to have a *roommate* and what *location* you would like, then start looking for the apartment.

Probably the best way of finding an apartment is through the grapevine. Just about everyone you meet in Manhattan lives in an apartment and has an inside line on vacancies in his or her building. Begin your search by putting out the word among friends and friends of friends that you're in the market. There is quite a turnover in apartments in the city, and frequently the landlord doesn't have to advertise.

Scan the newspapers, especially the Sunday *New York Times* real estate section. Try to get a copy of this section from a newsstand on the preceding Thursday or Friday. If you wait until Sunday, most of the bargain apartments will be taken.

The *Village Voice* is a weekly that has good apartment listings—so good, in fact, that you practically have to grab the first copy off the presses in order to get the best selection. If you want to make the effort, get yourself to the newsstand at Sheridan Square in Greenwich Village Wednesday morning.

In the dailies, many of the advertised apartments are handled through real estate agencies. If you go through an agency, either directly by calling one and asking them to look for you or by finding an apartment in an ad that is handled by an agency, expect to pay a fee of at least 10 percent (if you take the apartment).

If you know exactly which section of the city you prefer, you can always try a door-to-door check with superintendents. I have many friends who have done just that and been successful. However, this is a time-consuming and exhausting job and you may not have any luck.

Subletting is common in New York. The tenant wants to lease out his apartment to someone for a limited time. The sublet, for your protection, should be with the approval of the landlord. Ask to see the tenant's lease and look it over for provisions against subletting. The tenant may suggest that the landlord doesn't care one way or the other or won't find out about it anyway. If the tenant wants to handle the sublet himself, he can ask you to pay him directly. Many times he'll tack on an extra amount to his actual rental fee. Demand as official a document as possible with time and money agreements set down. But do be wary of the tenant who wants to sublet on the sly. When he or she leaves, you may face the consequences of an illegal rental situation.

If you don't mind sharing someone else's place, you can avoid the whole apartment search scene by looking for a roommate who comes with an apartment. Make sure to visit the potential roommate and his or her apartment before deciding on anything. Go to the same bulletin boards mentioned earlier in the roommate section, look through the papers for ads, place an ad yourself, or go to one of the roommate services.

Landlords and Leases

When you find an apartment that meets your price, size, condition, and location demands, take it. Act quickly when you know the apartment is what you want. Too often, apartments are lost because the would-be tenant decides to "think about it." Landlords are notoriously fickle and they usually have a long line of prospective renters at their door.

Will the "super" or landlord who shows you the apartment ask for or expect something under the table? Possibly. Sometimes, they will come right out with it and blatantly demand a month's rent for themselves. The only indication may be a strange hesitancy to say yes to your bid. There is no predicting how a super will act; this petty extortion is common, but not universal. Know if you are willing and able to fork over a bribe for an apartment and be prepared to lose one if you are not. Remember that you'll have to come up with one month's security rent and one month's advance rent and possibly a realty fee. If you can't squeeze out more for the super or landlord and if he or she won't be charmed out of avarice, don't despair. Keep looking—eventually you'll find another place.

Landlords love quiet, well-groomed, prosperous-looking tenants. They don't want any trouble or noise, just their money. When you meet them, try to give the impression of financial security and dress for your grandmother. If possible, avoid mentioning that you are an actor or acting student. Some landlords hear "actor" and immediately see the dollar signs disintegrating. You can be a regular student usually, because the landlord will assume mom and dad will help out. Don't lie, but don't say more than you have to. Just leave the landlord confident that you are respectful, neat, solvent, and an angel.

Most leases are for one to three years in duration. Of course, you should assure the landlord that you plan to stay at least as long as the lease stipulates. If you do move before the lease expires, you will probably lose the month's security you put down.

Before you have found a place to live, take time to visit one of the tenants' associations in the city, such as the Tenants' Union of the West Side, 262 West 81st Street, 212—595—1274. (Call first; the office is only staffed two days a week.) Ask them to explain leases, the necessity of having one and what all the small print means. Ask for any materials they have that describe landlord/tenant responsibilities and rights and the names of city housing agencies that handle tenant complaints. They can also explain the current rent laws of the city, what you can expect to pay in increases, and how to find out if the landlord is charging a fair rent.

There is a lot to know about leases and landlord/tenant relationships. Better if you can be forearmed with this knowledge before you sign anything.

SETTLING IN

No one has to tell you that the cost of living has sky-rocketed. Rentals, food and drug prices, clothing, and entertainment costs are high all over the country and New York is no exception. But there are still some bargains in the city and reasonable prices for food and clothing and entertainment can be found, if you know where to look.

You've seen how rentals can vary in the city. The same is true of just about every marketable item. Try to become an informed buyer. *Consumer's Report,* a monthly periodical sold for $1.00 at newsstands, runs informative articles and has a special December Buying Guide available for $2.65. Write Back Issue Department, Consumer's Union, Orangeburg, New York 10962. Another helpful publication is *Consumer Guide,* available at newsstands and by subscription; *Consumer Guide,* 3323 West Main Street, Skokie, Illinois 60076.

Budgeting in New York

Your most immediate buying needs will be food, drugs, a few household items, and possibly some furniture and clothing. (Try to bring along as complete a wardrobe from home as you can manage. For the first few months, you'll have enough other staples to worry about.)

Food

Food is all over the place in New York. Every conceivable taste treat from mangoes and persimmons to McDonald's and Kentucky Fried is available. Since you won't be living exclusively on Big Macs and Baskin-Robbins, you should know some basics on economic food shopping.

Even if you live in a dormitory or residence with meals included, eventually you'll start buying your own food. If you are in an acting school, you can follow the crowds to the local luncheonette or delicatessen. There probably will be a convenient quick-food place near your school or in your neighborhood. But, eventually, your stomach will crave a little variety and your budget may insist that you start grocery shopping and bringing your own lunch or cooking your own breakfast and dinner. It may be easier to eat out, but in the long run, it is a faster drain on your budget.

The cheapest grocery stores in New York are the big supermarket chains. Specialty stores, delicatessens, and small food markets cater to last-minute buyers who will pay any price. Usually, these smaller food stores will jack up the price of everyday items at least a few cents more than the supermarket. For select items such as fresh pastrami or nuts, some foreign foods, and so forth, these specialty stores are excellent. But for everyday food and household needs (soap, toilet paper, paper towels, cleansers, floor wax, and the like) the supermarkets offer the best prices.

Even the chain store prices vary. Some cater to a posher trade, that is, because they are in a more expensive neighborhood, they charge more. The same chain will charge more in its east Eighties' branch than in its West-Side store across town. Not only are there differences from section to section, but also within the same neighborhood. Within a few blocks on the West Side, for example, you'll find two large chain stores who underprice each other on certain items. One will have cheaper meat prices, the other cheaper canned goods and produce. Whatever section you choose for shopping, presumably it will be near your apartment, do some comparison shopping in the various supermarkets and find where the bargains are. You'll find yourself very resentful when one day you see tomatoes at 49¢ a pound when you've been paying 89¢ just a block away.

Neighborhood fresh fruit, fish, and meat markets sometimes offer a wider selection, better quality, and lower prices than the supermarkets. There is no standard rule. However, these small fresh-food markets deserve a look—they are charming and full of character, but they can be exorbitant as well.

On some good weather days, you may be lucky enough to pass a makeshift street vegetable/fruit vendor. He has gotten hold of a shipment and wants to move it fast. (He probably doesn't have a peddler's license and he has to sell out before the police see him.) If the quality and price are good—they usually are—snap up the bargain while it lasts.

Pharmaceuticals

Throughout the city you can find several discount drugstores. Again, search out the bargains. Today I can buy a fourteen-ounce name-brand deodorant for $2.89 at a normal drugstore in my neighborhood. A few blocks away at a discount drugstore, I can find the same brand, same size, for $2.29.

Large dime-store chains such as Woolworth's and Lamston's and some supermarkets also have cheap prices on nonprescription drugs.

When you have to fill a prescription and the discount store you frequent doesn't have a licensed pharmacist, go to a couple of regular drugstores and see which will give you the cheaper price. You will get the same pills or medicine called for in your prescription at every drugstore, but since there is no law yet on the books controlling markups, you will not always get the same price. Don't hesitate to ask the price before you tell them to fill the prescription and don't be shy about asking them to return it unfilled. People do this frequently. The drugs are sold for profit and, as the consumer, it is your right to find the better buy.

Some large department stores such as Macy's and Alexander's carry both prescription and nonprescription drugs. They have good prices and credit-card shopping. (Information on opening charge accounts will appear later in this chapter.)

Household Items

Many household needs (scrub brushes, brooms, mops, glasses, pans, extension cords, and the like) are available in neighborhood hardware stores, discount department stores, and dime stores. Every section of New York has its own shopping mall. You won't have to go far from your apartment to locate a variety of stores. The busiest streets of the neighborhood, such as Broadway and Amsterdam on the upper West Side and First and Second Avenue on the East Side, are teeming with hardware and dime stores, laundromats, shoe repair shops, cleaners, florists, and so forth.

Household items can also be purchased cheaply in large department stores such as Korvettes, Macy's, and Alexander's. However, you may find it too cumbersome to lug large items home by bus or subway when you can get the same things in one of your neighborhood stores.

Furniture

Furniture can be gotten cheaply in New York if you know where to go. The only item you may want to buy new is a mattress. Best buys on mattresses are in big department stores such as Macy's and Alexander's. Neighborhood discount stores may not deliver or have what you need in stock. Wherever you buy, be sure to ask how long you'll have to wait for delivery.

Many people use a large piece of foam rubber as a mattress, placed in a loft bed or homemade frame. Foam rubber mattresses are comfortable and can be bought in varying degrees of hardness. Certainly foam rubber is cheaper. You can go to Canal Rubber Supply, 329 Canal Street (CA6–7339), for good prices and advice.

For the essential pieces, consider buying used furniture. Several secondhand stores are scattered throughout Manhattan and they have a variety of styles to choose from. The stores tend to cluster together; on the upper West Side, for example, most are located along Columbus and Amsterdam Avenues, with a few on Broadway.

These bargain shops carry, as you will see, just about everything. Besides furniture, you can find lamps, mirrors, picture frames, dishes, eating utensils, and so on. They usually have a fast turnover of merchandise. They tend to be cluttered, and good items can be hidden away under a junk pile. So go prepared to scavenge and buy on the spot. Consider how you can transport heavier items home—see if the store delivers. Always, when buying furniture and large items, bring your room and door measurements with you and check the size of would-be purchases with them. Bargain furniture can be a boon to your budget and even your decor, but the items are not new and may be too wobbly or even beyond repair. Give a realistic appraisal of their sturdiness and durability before you buy.

One last source of secondhand furniture, available for free

to any discriminating scavenger, is the street. Many people scout blocks for furniture discarded on the sidewalk, left for the garbage pickup. Much left outside is beyond hope, but occasionally you will come across a gem, usually in the high-income neighborhoods. The Department of Sanitation picks up large items regularly. Call them to find out when they pick up in your neighborhood or in the neighborhood where you want to hunt and get there before them.

Clothing

Ideas on what to wear for auditions, job interviews, and so on will be discussed in a later chapter. Your immediate clothing needs can be served cheaply and even fashionably if you know where to buy.

Acting students dress for comfort and easy mobility. Dungarees or some variation on the "work clothes" look are the old standbys. The work clothes stores on Canal Street in the lower Village have the best prices and a large selection. Ordinary army-navy stores, long popular for their good prices (pea jackets have always been a bargain), can be found on Manhattan, mainly in blue-collar neighborhoods such as the Lower East Side.

If you take any kind of movement or dance class, you'll need at least a couple of leotards and tights and ballet slippers or sneakers. (Tap or jazz shoes if you take either of these.) When buying shoes, get the most comfortable, best-fitting ones you can find. *Capezio* Shops at 1612 Broadway (at 49th Street) and 177 MacDougal (West Village) or *Selva* at 1607 Broadway have an excellent selection of dance footwear.

Sneakers can be found anywhere, but invest in a pair of good quality. Whatever shoes you buy should be well-supported and durable. If this means spending more, do. New York is hard on feet and actors walk even more than most people. (Equity offers a free pair of shoes to Union members. Details in a later chapter.)

Leotards and tights (find out if your class calls for bare feet; if so, buy footless tights) don't have to be perfect fits.

You can get irregulars for a discount at small hosiery stores such as *BuyWell* at 2357 and 2592 Broadway. *Herbet's* at 1657 Broadway (between 51st and 52nd) on the third floor has dance wear usually a dollar or so cheaper than retail.

If you have a yen for dressing up occasionally and you can't afford the prices at Bloomingdale's, Saks, or Bonwit Teller (some of the classier department stores), or at any of the hundreds of boutiques around town, have a look at stores such as Ohrbach's which sells many name brands for less than you'd pay elsewhere. You might like to visit the Flea Market of New York—Orchard Street—located in lower Manhattan. There are about three hundred stores in this seven-block area with goods piled high and bulging racks both inside stores and out on the sidewalk. The discounts average around 25 percent, but on higher quality items, the reductions may be only a few dollars. You can find just about any kind of clothing or accessory on Orchard Street and, if you can cope with the crowds, especially on Sundays, and the frenzy, if you have good bargain instincts (the quality of goods is erratic), you'll probably have a successful shopping spree.

Secondhand clothing stores for more exotic, unusual, and sometimes cheaper fashions, abound in Manhattan. Several are located in the Village, East and West, and uptown, East and West sides. Since these stores have become chic, you may find some of them ridiculously expensive. The look of the clientele may be a giveaway. Search out the more remote stores, avoiding high-income, tourist-trap areas. Ninth Avenue on the West Side in the Fifties has a string of secondhand clothing stores of the cluttered variety. But you can still dig out a classy outfit if you have the patience to wade through piles of clothing.

If you sew and can get your hands on a machine (maybe in the costume shop of your school), you'll find a tremendous selection of materials at the fabric shops on Orchard Street.

Transportation

Getting from one place to another in New York is easy and still cheap. The subway and bus fares as of 1975 are fifty

cents a trip. Buses don't offer transfers, but many of them
follow such wide-ranging routes that you can get from one
side of town to another, from uptown to downtown and vice
versa all in one trip.

Since New York traffic is usually jammed during daylight
hours, buses are sometimes slow. As a rule, the stops are
every two blocks and the bus will not pick up or let out
passengers except at these designated corners. When you first
arrive in New York, ride several different buses just to
familiarize yourself with the city. If you can't afford the time
to ride for the sake of riding, schedule your day so that you
can get where you're going by bus. By allowing a little more
time for a bus ride, you can speed up your learning the
layout of Manhattan.

Subways are fast but not very pleasant to your senses.
They are noisy, ugly, sometimes smelly and dirty—and they
are indispensable. New York lends itself to hurrying. For
some reason, appointments and classes and auditions frequently run into one another and you will have only a few
minutes for traveling. On those days, you can be saved by the
subway.

Approximately four million people ride the subway daily.
Most of them are on the trains during the rush hours, 7 a.m.
to 10 a.m. and 4 p.m. to 7 p.m. If possible, avoid these times.
If not, just accept the fact that for the duration of your trip
you will be squeezed, shoved, and breathed on. The same
thing happens on buses during rush hours, except that it lasts
longer.

Besides speed, subways offer transfers from one train to
another often without the need of another token. Subways
usually stop every seven to ten blocks within the boundaries
of Manhattan. Most trains terminate in other boroughs. Express trains, usually available across the tracks from the
locals, stop only at the busiest stations. Express stops on the
West Side are at Chambers Street, West 4th Street, 14th
Street, 34th Street (near Penn Central and Macy's), 42nd
Street (Times Square), 72nd Street, 96th Street, 125th
Street, and on into the Bronx; on the East Side they are at
14th Street, Grand Central, 59th Street, 86th Street, and
125th Street.

One last bit of information: Subways and buses offer two rides for the price of one on Saturday evenings, Sundays, and holidays. For any other bus and subway travel information, call 212—330—1234.

Cabs are outrageously expensive. Avoid them except in emergency situations and for your late-night safety.

Transportation from the airports, Kennedy and LaGuardia into Manhattan, is provided by buses, cabs, and limousines. The Carey Bus Line charges $3.50 from Kennedy and $3.00 from LaGuardia. Their only termination point is the East Side Terminal, 308 East 38th Street. From there, you will have to get other transportation to your destination. Cabs run by meter and the fare from LaGuardia is usually $8—$12, from Kennedy, $10—$15. Limousines (group, not private) carry about five passengers, charge $10—$12 from Kennedy, $5—$7 from LaGuardia, and will take you to your door. (Price range takes into account traffic flow and various termination points in Manhattan.) All cab and limousine drivers expect at least a 15 to 20 percent gratuity.

Medical and Dental Care

Doctors and dentists in New York can charge from $15 to $100 per office visit, exclusive often of special services such as laboratory tests, injections, construction of inlay, and the like.

Get the names of an *internist* (most doctors in New York are specialists), who can act as a general physician and refer you to any specialist you might need, and a regular *dentist*. Friends usually can suggest a doctor or you can call a university health service, such as Columbia's or New York University's; tell them you are one of their students and ask them to recommend a doctor. These services keep lists of reputable and reasonably priced physicians for such requests from students. Even if you don't have an immediate need for medical or dental attention, it is a good idea to have a name and number for any emergency treatment or referral. You can ask the nurse what the doctor's fees usually run. Sometimes a doctor in Manhattan will have two offices, one on the East Side and one on the West Side. Usually, he or she charges West Side patients less, so call the West Side office for information and appointments.

Find out where the nearest free health clinic is located. You may want to use its services on occasion. Manhattan has eight such centers:

> Central Harlem, 2238 5th Avenue, 690–2600
> East Harlem, 158 East 115th Street, 876–0300
> Lower East Side, 341 East 25th Street, 689–6353
> Lower West Side, 303 9th Avenue, 524–2537
> Manhattanville, 21 Old Broadway, 666–5900
> Morningside, 264 West 118th Street, 663–3822
> Riverside, 160 West 100th Street, 866–2500
> Washington Heights, 600 West 168th Street, 927–6300

The centers provide a variety of services, including immunization, cancer detection tests, VD tests, pregnancy tests, and so on. Call the one nearest you for a rundown of their services.

Manhattan also has various free counseling services. For abortion, birth control, and gynecological advice and referral, call a Planned Parenthood office. For free cancer tests information, call the American Cancer Society at 586–8700.

The city also provides neighborhood health fair clinics at various times of the year. For details on dates and locations of these fairs, which offer a battery of free tests, call the American Cancer Society at 586–8700.

For private psychiatric counseling and therapy, call one of the university health services for referral. Usually private fees are about $25 to $50 for a 45-to-50-minute session. If you cannot afford private care, look into some of the low-cost psychiatric services offered by clinics such as the following:

> Alfred Adler Mental Hygiene Clinic
> 333 Central Park West
> 663–7980

> Fifth Avenue Center for Counseling and Psychotherapy,
> Inc.
> 10 West 10th Street
> 989–2990

Hudson Guild
   441 West 26th Street
   760–9800

Karen Horney Clinic, Inc.
   329 East 62nd Street
   838–4333

Metropolitan Center for Mental Health
   336 Central Park West
   850–7000

New York Psychoanalytic Institute
   247 East 82nd Street
   879–6900

New York State Psychiatric Institute
   722 West 168th Street
   568–4000

Postgraduate Center for Mental Health
   124 East 28th Street
   689–7700

William Alanson White Institute of Psychiatry, Psycho-
   analysis and Psychology
   20 West 74th Street
   873–7070

Insurance

The best insurance plans for actors are those offered by the unions, AFTRA, Equity, and SAG. Details on the coverage offered members are discussed in a later chapter.

Until you can get this union group coverage and if you no longer are covered in your parents' policy, call a large, well-established company such as Allstate, State Farm, Mutual of Omaha, or Hartford Life. They will be happy to advise you on health insurance plans.

The Emerging New Yorker

Estimate how much it will cost you to live in the city, following the loose guidelines of the following budgets. Maybe

Estimated Annual Budgets for Full-Time
Acting Student Living in Dormitory or Residence

	Minimum	Maximum
Tuition	$1,415	$3,300
Room and Board	$1,600	$2,600
Supplies	$ 100	$ 350
Personal	$ 400	$ 750
Total	$3,515	
Approximate Average	$5,000	$7,000

For Full-time Acting Student with Apartment

	Minimum	Maximum
Tuition	$1,415	$ 3,300
Rent	$1,500 (realistic low)	$ 3,000 (medium high)
Phone, Electric, and Gas	$ 240	$ 560
Food	$1,800 (eating in)	$ 2,500 (eating in)
		$ 3,600 (eating out only)
Transportation	$ 250	$ 350
Miscellaneous	$ 800	$ 1,000
Total	$6,005	$10,710–$11,810
Approximate Average	$8,500	

you can eliminate some expenses and/or add on a few of your own. Whatever figure you come up with will probably be less than you will spend. For safety, tack on an extra fifty dollars a month and try to gather together a good portion of the total before you come to the city. Even if you plan to get a full- or part-time job (see following discussion), you'll feel much more secure with a sizeable checking account. Besides, you may not want to work while studying, or you may not be able to find a job right away.

Come with enough money in traveler's checks (avoid bringing a large amount of cash) to last until you are able to open a checking account in the city. You may not want to choose a bank until you find an apartment. Even if you plan to live in a dormitory or residential hotel and you immediately open an account, expect a few weeks' delay in banking services. Usually, New York banks require a clearance period of ten days to two weeks before you can write checks on a new account.

Do not expect to cash out-of-town checks in New York, unless your school provides such a service. You usually can pay rent and certain bills with out-of-town checks, but few merchants or service managers will accept them. You may be able eventually to cash a check or pay for purchases in your neighborhood when you establish yourself as a regular customer. For the first few weeks, however, have an alternate means of getting ready cash. (A Master Charge, Bank Americard, American Express Card, or the like, if you have one, will do.)

Charge Accounts

To open a charge account in New York, you must earn $100 per week or the yearly equivalent. Students and freelance professionals (such as actors) sometimes have difficulty opening charge accounts. One alternative is to have your mother or father open an account that authorizes you to use the card.

Temporary Employment

If you have to find nonacting work to support yourself, look for a job with flexible hours—either part-time, or full-time employment on a temporary basis.

Follow the same procedures in job-hunting as in apartment-hunting. Ask friends for leads, look at bulletin boards, scan the newspapers' classified sections. Definitely look through the trades, *Backstage* and *Show Business*. You'll find actor-oriented part-time jobs and temporaries' agencies who cater to actors. The agencies offer a variety of jobs. Call several and find out which provides the best pay, the most appealing work, the most flexibility.

The typical agency will tell you to come in for an interview and/or a skills test (in typing, for example), will fill out a card with your available hours and skills, and will explain how they operate. They will call you when a job comes up which may be for one or two days, a week, a month, possibly longer. You can accept or refuse at will. Too many refusals will probably mean fewer calls.

If you want to check out the credentials of any agency or potential employer, call the Better Business Bureau at 989–7600.

To find a job somehow connected with theatre, television, or film, you'll have to depend on your connections. Most of these jobs, such as helping out at auditions, working in an advertising agency, producer's office, costume shop, and so on, are given to friends or friends of friends. The work is not glamorous or necessarily helpful to your career. Remember, you are not hired as an actor. However, you may pick up some useful behind-the-scenes information.

Consider carefully whether or not you would accept a job "off the books." This means that the employer would pay you without taking out any money for taxes or benefits. Of course, you would get more money, but when the job ends you would not be able to use it toward collecting unemployment insurance. Be sure that any job "on the books" does pay into the government's unemployment funds, besides taking out the usual amount for taxes and social security.

Unemployment Insurance

New York State offers a high rate of unemployment insurance that has helped many actors through difficult financial stretches. To qualify, as of 1975, you must have worked during at least twenty of the weeks of the fifty-two weeks before filing (one day's acting work, commercial or film shoot, or soap opera taping will count as one week of work). You must have earned at least $600 in *covered* earnings, that is, your employer must have paid into government unemployment funds for you.

You cannot have left your last job voluntarily without good cause. These are the basic qualifications you must meet before you can collect. For more information, call the New York State Unemployment Insurance office at 488–5406.

They will tell you whether or not you qualify and to which office to go for filing and collecting. Actors' unions have unemployment counselors who will advise members on their cases.

Enjoying New York Economically

Eating

You won't have trouble finding good, inexpensive restaurants in the city. Friends, various publications listing restaurants, and your own instincts are the best guides. The following are a few of the restaurants actors frequent—because of their low prices, friendly atmosphere, and proximity to the theatre districts. Occasionally, you might want to try one of these hangouts.

Restaurants

Charley O's, 33 West 48th Street
Haymarket, 772 8th Avenue
Jimmy Ray's, 729 8th Avenue
Joe Allen's, 326 West 46th Street
Pelican, 200 West 70th Street
Phoebe's Place, 361 Bowery
Piccadilly Hotel Coffee Shop, 227 West 45th Street
Sardi's, 234 West 44th Street (more expensive)

Underground Nightclub Circuit

Brothers and Sisters, 355 West 46th Street
Grande Finale, 210 West 70th Street
Reno Sweeney's, 126 West 13th Street

Theatre

Theatre tickets for most Broadway shows can be gotten at discount prices from the Ticket Center box office in Duffy Square at 47th Street and Broadway. Some theatres sell discount tickets to students with certified identification cards. Frequently, long-running shows not playing to full houses will offer "twofers," discount tickets that let two people in for the price of one. You can find them in schools, restaurants, and stores throughout Manhattan. Sometimes shows that are sellouts will offer a limited number of Standing Room Only tickets at low prices. Call the theatre and find out when these tickets go on sale—first come, first served usually. If you want to take your chances on a new show in previews, the preopening period before reviews, you often can get tickets at reduced prices.

As an actor or acting student, you will frequently have a chance to get free theatre tickets. Professional schools, teachers, friends in shows, often have access to free seats. Many times, shows in previews paper their houses by channeling gratis tickets through theatre schools. Keep your eyes and ears open and you can see many shows free of charge.

The best places to find out about other free entertainment in Manhattan are the "Calendar of Events" sections of newspapers, periodicals such as *New York Magazine*, and neighborhood publications such as *Wisdom's Child*, the *Westsider*, the *Soho News, Manhattan East*, or the *East Side Herald*, available for delivery or at their neighborhood newsstands. They list everything from art exhibits and musical performances to lectures and poetry readings and folk dancing. You'll find that New York, especially in the summer, offers a rich variety of free entertainment—Shakespeare in the Park, the Schaefer Music Festival, Lincoln Center Outdoor Concerts, and many others.

Personal Safety

At Home

See that your apartment door has at least two good locks. It is smart to put in a new cylinder (the center portion of a lock where the key is inserted) when you first move in. In this way, you can be sure of the number of keys and of who has them. A popular cylinder on the market today, difficult to pick and recommended by most locksmiths, is the *Medeco*. Because it takes longer to pick than other cylinders, it may discourage burglars. Most locksmiths recommend that the lock itself be a dead-bolt lock (requires a key to lock) and that you put a guard plate over the exposed cylinder to prevent its being ripped out of the door.

A deterrent to jimmying a door with a crowbar is a right-angle metal strip, secured by bolts to the meeting point of frame and door. See if your landlord will install this for you. Landlords, by the way, do not always take kindly to these requests because they don't want to put out the money or they dislike marking up the door. Play it by ear with your landlord; try to cajole him or her into helping you or at least allowing you to pay for alterations. If he or she refuses, take the initiative and call in a good locksmith. You have a right to protect yourself and your home.

Definitely be sure your apartment entry door has a peephole. *Never* allow any unknown, unexpected caller inside your door, be he a repairman, telephone man, messenger, survey taker, salesman, someone who is lost, or whoever. If your apartment building doesn't have an intercom system, set up a buzz code with your friends. When they visit, have them always use the code—one long buzz, two short, for example.

To repeat, do not unlock your door for any stranger who comes unannounced or unrequested. If it is a package delivery, ask the person to leave it outside your door. If your signature is required, ask that the paper be slipped under the door. For legitimate repair or installment visits or package deliveries, find out the day, if not the exact time, when you can expect the service. Most gas and electric meters are not in apartments, but in the basement. If you have a meter in your apartment, you can call Con Edison and find out the week when the reading will be made. New York is full of very imaginative, extremely convincing con men. Don't be a victim.

Every police precinct has a security and crime-prevention department. You can call your precinct and ask for a free security check on your apartment and building. They can advise you and your landlord on necessary safety measures.

When you enter your building, have your key ready and do not let strangers in with you. If necessary, turn around and leave the building before you unlock the main entrance. Avoid getting into an elevator with someone you don't recognize. If you are on the elevator and someone suspicious gets on, get out on that floor or stay by the control board so you can get to the emergency button if necessary.

If you spot a stranger in the halls or suspect someone who rings your bell, alert other tenants or the landlord. You may want to call the police.

If you should come home one day and notice something suspicious—your apartment door ajar, a light shining under the door when you know you didn't leave it on, or the like—don't go inside. You may be unlucky enough to catch the burglar in the act. Immediately get the super to check out the apartment. If you have been burglarized, call the police. While you're waiting, make a list of missing possessions. (The police suggest that you have valuables indelibly marked with a number for easy identification. Call your local precinct for information.) When the police arrive, they will question you and advise you on what precautions to take and what to hope for in retrieved items (not much).

The best precaution against break-in, abuse, or mugging in your apartment or building is to make a habit of being alert and vigilant at all times.

Safety on the Streets

You can avoid harassment and abuses on the street by following a few commonsense rules. Avoid walking alone at night on strange, deserted, poorly lit streets. (If necessary, walk in the center of the street, not on the sidewalk.) If you attend the theatre or movies, you'll be exiting with the crowds and most entertainment centers are in busy, night-life districts. Ask neighbors about the advisability of solo night walks in your neighborhood or returning late and alone from an evening out. If they say it is not safe to walk alone at night, don't. And try to take cabs to your door if you return late and the bus or subway stops are quite a distance from your apartment. If you don't want to pay for a taxi for the entire distance, you can take a bus or subway to a busy stop close to your apartment and catch a cab for the last few blocks. Taxis are available and can be flagged down all day long and well into the night and early morning on most main thoroughfares.

If you're alone visiting friends, ask them to walk you to the nearest bus or subway stop or to wait until you catch a cab.

If, for some reason, you should be caught outside alone at night and sense that you are in danger, move quickly to the closest store or busy, well-lit street or to a passerby for shelter and help. Don't run into an apartment building—you can't be sure of entry and it is better to avoid enclosed, empty hallways if you are being followed.

Purse- and wallet-snatchers and pickpockets work day and night throughout Manhattan. One protection against them is to have a bag that closes securely with no open pouches containing anything valuable. Don't put money or wallets in side or back pockets and avoid carrying large amounts of cash, if possible, at all times. (Some people like to have at least five or ten dollars ready to pacify a mugger, rather than provoke him by having very little.) A bag with sturdy strap, carried with a firm grip close to the body, discourages snatchers who sense that you are alert and not an easy mark. Men, put wallets and identification and credit cards into your breast or inside pockets.

Don't ever leave any belongings unattended in a restaurant or public place. Don't leave suitcases, bicycles, or other items on the street unwatched and don't leave anything visible to passersby inside an empty locked car.

If you're cautious, you can avoid serious difficulties on the streets. The only disturbances you probably will have to face are peddlers or winos asking for change or, if you are a woman, various catcalls, remarks, clucks, and assorted animal noises. The best reaction is no reaction. Just keep walking.

Transportation Safety

Subways and buses are not dangerous—with a few exceptions to the rule. Very late at night, subway stations may be deserted and you will be better off staying above ground and taking a bus or a cab.

Occasionally, pickpockets work city buses. They usually prey on men, going for the back pocket, and work in pairs during rush hour. One man creates a distraction and the other lifts the wallet or purse. Watch out for suspicious-looking characters and stay at the other end of the bus.

Sometimes young people ride in between the cars of a subway and grab for the purse or packages of a disembarking passenger as the train pulls out of the station. Avoid this by moving toward the center of the platform.

As you assimilate, you'll gradually discover the ups and downs of New York City living. Despite the crime and abuse and annoyance, it is not all bad. There is a concomitant freedom to act as you please with anonymity and to see what only New York can show you—just about everything under the sun.

CHAPTER 3

Breaking In: The Equipment

PICTURES

The most important first step you take as you walk out of your training period is into a photographer's studio. By this time you've heard about pictures and résumés. They may have an exaggerated importance in the business, but they are essential. Before you can do any kind of auditioning as a professional you must have pictures and résumés. To walk into an interview or audition without them is amateurish and your chances of making a good impression are practically zero. Even if the interviewers like you enough to call you back, without a picture of you for remembrance and a résumé with some vital contact information you'll never survive in their memories amidst the hundreds of other faces.

Getting photographs is expensive. You probably won't get away with paying less than $50.00—and that is a very low estimate. There are alternatives to going the normal route of finding a good photographer, sitting for him, collecting your pictures, and paying anywhere from $50.00 to $150.00, prices of extra copies included. The first of these alternatives is getting a friend to take pictures of you. Usually this shortcut is a waste of time. Most friends who like to take pictures haven't the equipment, experience, or devotion to produce top-notch professional photos. Unless your friend happens to be a professional photographer, he or she probably won't get the best results. Of course there are exceptions. If you decide you don't have that much to lose by letting your friend try, just remember that you may have to take on half the work yourself: buying the film, getting the rolls to a laboratory for development, paying for the enlargements and the touch-ups that you must request. In short, there's more to getting photographs taken by a friend than just posing for them. After all the extra effort, you may not like the results and you'll be back where you started. Remember, professional photographers have an eye for setting up good shots—that's their business, and usually that extra instinct is what makes the difference between the work of a friend and the work of a professional.

The other alternative to paying a photographer's fee is going around to various studios and seeing if you can interest any of the photographers in taking a test roll of you. Even if the photographer isn't interested in using you for any modeling, he or she will usually give you the contact sheet consisting of the developed unenlarged frames of one or two rolls of film. The cost is minimal for the photographer who has a little free time and is always looking for interesting subjects.

Do you have to be gorgeous and stunning for free photos? Well, it would certainly not work against you, but good photographers are intrigued by many kinds of faces and, if they respond to you personally, chances are they'll go ahead and shoot a roll.

A word of caution: Some photographers may not ask for any money, but they have been known to request other kinds of payment. I once was in need of new pictures and short of funds, so I decided to try what I've just described. To my surprise the first photographer I dropped in on was quite friendly and seemed anxious to do business with me as a model. I felt unthreatened initially because we were in his studio, which was well equipped and in a respectable office building on one of New York's more elegant blocks. The excessive warmth and interest in my career that he showed should have been a tip-off. But not until we had chatted for over an hour and he had taken me into the shooting room and taken one roll of pictures, did I catch on. That's when he asked if I was ready to try a few shots without my clothes. By that time I had built up enough of an invisible defense line to be able to get out of the situation with some grace and without undressing. He was quite pleasant about my refusal to strip, as he put it, it just depended on what kind of modeling I was interested in. He even offered to enlarge two or three of the pictures he had already taken. When I came to get them in a few days—with a friend in tow—he handed them over with no strings and also no offers for modeling work. The end of the story is that one of the shots was excellent and I used it for a year or so.

Not every photographer will put you through this kind of scene, but you should be aware—particularly if you are a woman—of the possibility. If you want to try and get free test shots, probably the best approach is through a friend who knows a photographer interested in finding models and whose name you can use. Call first and ask if you can come in sometime. If you have no connections you can just go to the yellow pages and call a few studios. If they are interested in testing models they'll let you know and tell you to drop by. This phone call usually saves time and also some embarrassment at walking in unannounced to a studio at a busy time when the photographer is preoccupied. If you don't have pictures or money, this method is certainly worth trying. If you're professional about it, the photographer will be also.

The easiest method of getting good pictures is the normal way—paying a fee and letting the photographer do the work. Before you select one, look over pictures of other actors. If you see a good shot ask for the photographer's name. You'll find a variety of styles and a preponderance of head shots. Head shots are more useful for an actor because body shots are not of much interest to casting people except in a portfolio, which you don't have to worry about at this point. (More on portfolios later in this chapter.)

A good photograph looks like the subject. If you can't

recognize the person from his or her picture, what good is it? Too often vanity or fantasy gets in the way of common sense and actors are tempted to select pictures that they think flatter them or present a glamorous side that is not apparent in a face-to-face interview. A casting director confronted by this contrast between idealized photo and physical reality laughs up his sleeve and won't bother keeping you in mind. He wants the picture because it tells him what you look like, for later reference. If your photographs don't do just that, they are no help to you. Don't sell short the way you look—if you don't like it, then fix it up before you get your pictures taken. Don't expect the photographer to be your groomer and makeup artist, your hairdresser and clothes designer. If you go into the studio looking your best, with a few different hair styling ideas in mind (wigs don't photograph too well), changes of jacket, shirt, blouse, or sweater or a pair of glasses, perhaps (jewelry for either sex isn't usually a good idea), the photographer will do his part. He'll find the different sides of your personality and, hopefully, bring out various moods and expressions that show you as you. Good photographs, if they do nothing else, tell a person what he or she looks like. Make sure you're happy with that and you should be able to distinguish and select the good shots on your contact sheets.

When you get the names of several photographers you think might be good—from the usual sources, by the way, actor friends, the trades—call and ask if you can stop by and look at their work. Photographers keep stacks of pictures just for this purpose. They don't and shouldn't expect you to make any commitment at this point. Tell them you'll let them know for sure in a few days.

Look for nonromanticized, nonstylized real pictures. Of course it would help if friends had work done by the various photographers you are considering. If they produce pictures that look like your friends, you know they meet the reality requirement. Look for natural poses and facial expressions and for well-lit photos, that don't cast shadows on the faces of subjects. The best shots, besides looking like you, should be frontal or three-quarter. Profile shots are not appreciated by casting people except perhaps in a portfolio. Neither are distraction shots that show you with hair over one eye or in any other gimmicky pose. Character shots are okay as long as they look like you—don't "character" yourself out of recognition—and as long as you have normal shots along with them.

A good photographer should be able to give you a variety of shots that you could use for theatre, television, film, or commercial interviews and auditions. Theatrical shots can be a bit serious and dramatic or comic and characterlike. Television, film, and commercial photographs should have a minimum of mood imposition. The best commercial shot is straightforward, pleasant-faced, alive, and real. If you have character work possibilities don't be heavy-handed about it—looking cross-eyed, having a cigar hanging out of your mouth, showing a gap in your front teeth. Casting people looking for character types want real-looking characters and they don't need to be hit over the head with your comic or villainous possibilities. If you're fat and jolly or gaunt and dark and that's what they want, they'll see it in a regular shot. In other words, the best thing you have going for you in a photograph is that it sells you as you, whether youth, ingenue, romantic lead, or character type. It is important of course that you know which of these categories you fit and that you accentuate them in your photos. Casting is done by type—face that reality, please—and then work within the present limits of your potential.

If you want to do commercials, you must give yourself a type analysis before you get pictures. Watch several commercials and break down the actors of your sex into however many different types you can distinguish. Then decide which of these types you fit. Ask advice from friends or professionals such as agents or casting directors. You cannot see yourself from the outside, and you can never be as objective about yourself as you might like to think.

When you know which category you fit, go to your photographer looking like a "typical type." If you are having more than just commercial shots taken, bring along a change of clothes or some accessories and tell the photographer you want to use them when he or she takes your commercial shots. Nothing too elaborate is necessary: for instance, if you are a young male with a clean-cut collegiate look, you could bring along a bow tie and horn-rimmed glasses. If you are a rugged outdoorsy type, a plaid sport shirt might do.

Women who are the young housewife type can use a button down blouse and a neat and conservative hairdo. A sex-kitten type might want to wear a low-cut or tight (within reason) top and a flouncier hair style.

Commercials are geared to speak to certain segments of the American public, and advertising agencies see that public in stereotype. The closer you approximate a stereotype in the pictures you submit for commercial work, the more likely you are to get auditions.

After you've looked over the work of several photographers and have found the ones who can give you the pictures you want, make your final selection according to personal preference. You should choose the photographer toward whom you feel friendly and with whom you can be relaxed. The rapport between photographer and subject is as important to good pictures as the camera. Don't compromise quality for good vibrations, but try to get the photographer who has both.

When you make the appointment, choose a day that is uncluttered with other activity. You want to look as rested, fit, and relaxed as possible. Be sure it's not so early in the day that you don't have enough time to fix yourself up or so late that your energy level is low. A good photography session is exhausting and can be as long as three or four hours.

You should find out ahead of time how many rolls of film the photographer will take; it should be at least four so that you'll have enough from which to choose. Also be sure that he or she will reshoot without charge if you can't find any shots you like from the first session. This is unlikely, but it doesn't hurt to get this assurance ahead of time.

Find out how much you get for your money. Some photographers charge a flat fee that includes equipment costs, sitting fee, and copies. Others charge separately for sitting and enlargements. Their low initial charge is misleading because enlargements can accelerate the bill to the same amount you'd pay in a flat fee. You may even pay beyond a flat fee if you want more than two or three enlargements. Photographers don't usually provide more than that number without charge. When you do have the contact sheet, try to stay within the limit of two or three selections. You only increase the cost by choosing more shots and you'll find that you won't be handing out more than two or three anyway. Choose the two or three shots that give distinctly different personas and still look like you. You'll find that you'll end up handing out the pictures that you prefer rather than what anyone else might like, so be sure the shots you choose are your favorites.

Some actors use composites—a regular 8 X 10 with three or four smaller pictures on it—rather than getting two or three individual shots. If you get a composite you should be sure it will work for you. Usually it's the kind of thing to give out at general interviews. For a specific audition and role, there will only be one picture that will be appropriate. Why confuse the situation with the rest of the composite? Probably, if you like the composite idea, it's best to get separate head shots along with it. The photographer will be able to advise you on this. Before you have photos taken, you might even ask some casting directors or agents you have occasion to meet what they prefer. This is a clever way you can ingratiate yourself with an agent, having made his or her acquaintance earlier and asking advice on your photos. You could, if you feel there is some interest, take in your contact sheet and ask for their choice of shots. You don't have to go along with their selections, but often they will take the time to help out and you have that much more of a relationship established.

After you have made your selections, gotten the enlargements, and satisfied yourself that they are what you want, go to a photo copy office such as Better Photo Service at 220 West 42nd Street or Ideal Photographic Corporation at 160 West 46th Street or Modernage Photographic Services at 6 West 48th Street or 319 East 44th, and get at least fifty glossies of each picture. Twenty-five is usually the least you can get, but that is often impractical because you'll go through that many in no time and the fewer you get the more you pay per picture. Better Photo charges $7.95 for twenty-five and $11.25 for fifty copies. If you don't have the enlargement negative, you'll have to pay $3.75 extra. The copy man will show you different styles—white-edged or bleed, name and number or not on the front. It's a good idea to have your name and telephone answering service number on the front of your picture, in case your résumé should get lost in the shuffle. Also, whoever sees your picture will immediately associate your face with your name. It usually takes three days to a week to get your copies.

Pictures are extremely important for actors. When you walk into any agent's or casting director's office, you'll see pictures up on the walls or files that are filled with photos. A picture may seem incidental to a personal interview but it is really a vital part. These casting people see thousands of applicants yearly, and the picture and résumé method is the only one yet in use that helps them remember you and call you back. Be sure the pictures you get do as much as they can to get you work.

RÉSUMÉS

The hardest part of writing up a résumé is getting yourself to sit down and do it. The form is simple enough—just be sure to look over several résumés and note all the essentials before you draw up your own.

What is the purpose of a résumé? Like pictures, it's part of your actor ID kit. When you walk into an interview or audition and sit down with a stranger who must make a decision about you or at least get as much information on your acting background as possible in five minutes, a good résumé is very helpful. Often the interviewer is only a collector of pictures and résumés. He or she delivers them into the hands of the director who has never met you and who makes audition decisions strictly on the merits of your picture and résumé. Believe it or not, that is often how selections are made. You have to put as much of you as possible into those two 8 X 10 sheets of paper, picture, and résumé, and hope they make a good impression.

What goes into a résumé? The first item is your name, placed in the center of the page, top line, in capital letters. Immediately below, list some of your identification marks:

home address and number (optional), service number, unions, height, age range, weight, hair color, and eye color.

Your acting credits should follow and take up the balance of the page. First make a list of all the plays and roles and any other theatrical, film, or commercial work—amateur or professional—that you have ever done. As soon as you are sure you've put everything down, begin eliminating. Résumés are not meant to be all-inclusive, but to impress the viewer with the range and quality of your work. Selectivity is important—too many parts clutter the page and look as if you have scraped bottom.

List theatre credits first. Top priority goes to any professional (paying) work in New York City. If you have no professional New York credits, you can use any showcase work in Off-Off-Broadway houses. If your professional school sponsored any productions open to the public you may include them. Next comes professional work outside New York—regional, summer stock, dinner theatre, university theatre (not as a student), and the like. If you don't have much professional work outside New York, list any amateur productions you've done: community theatre, club or service organization productions, children's theatre, and so on. Don't hesitate to include this kind of production if you have little or no professional work in or out of New York. You don't have to indicate the amateur status or other unnecessary information, just the name of the theatre where you performed. Who's to know if it was for the Elks or an old folks home? If there was no "theatre" involved, use your imagination and create a name for one. As long as you were in the show you list, you can exercise a little artistic license with the location. Don't go overboard; keep it amateur if it is so, because falsely listing it in any existing professional theatre, even though it may be hundreds of miles from New York, could be dangerous. Whoever reads your résumé may have just worked at that theatre or know someone who has.

Casting people don't try to trap you or put you through a cross-examination on the verity of your résumé. However, since items on the résumé are often the only things that you and the interviewer have in common, he or she may search it for a familiar play, theatre, or city and use it as a conversation starter. You'll often get questions such as "When were you there?" "Who directed?" "Where is that theatre located?" Never list anything that can accidentally trip you up and embarrass you and your interviewer.

After theatre credits list other professional work and, if you have enough in two or more media, keep them in separate sections. For instance, local or network television work, radio or television commercial spots, film work, singing work (concerts, opera, night club), or dancing.

For television work, list the show or job and the station call name and its national network affiliation, if any. For commercials, if you have done quite a few you may state "conflicts upon request." This means that you may not be sent up for an Excedrin commercial if you have a Bufferin commercial running, and the like. If you have only a few credits, then list the product, for example, "So-Good Dog Food," the ad agency, "Ed Baines agency," and the type: voice-over, extra, principal, special. (This last category, type, is optional.) For films list the title of the film, your role (name or extra or description), and the studio (Warners, Paramount, and so forth.)

One last section can be included, if you wish, briefly listing your training background, including acting, voice, movement and dance teachers, and special schools or courses such as commercial class, workshops, and so on.

When you have finished the lists and organized the format, type up a test draft. Make the form as neat, clean, and professional-looking as possible. Show your draft to some acting or directing friends or, better yet, to someone in casting who has seen hundreds of résumés and can make suggested alterations. When you type the final draft, try to do it on an electric typewriter. If you wish, for an extra charge (about $3.00) you can usually get the printer to whom you go for copies to type it up from your typed test draft. Be sure to leave enough space at the end of each section to allow typing in any work you get after the copies are made. You can't add on forever—as your career progresses you'll want to type up a new résumé—but leaving space for a few additions allows you to keep your résumé up to date.

Printing fees run from about $4.00 to $6.00 for 100 copies, $7.00 to $9.00 for 200 copies.

SAMPLE RÉSUMÉS

GEORGE GREEN

62 College Ave.
Apt. D-4, New York, N.Y.
Ser. Phone: PL7–6300

Height: 5'11"; Weight: 165
Eyes: Brown; Hair: Black
Age Range: 23–30
Unions: Equity, AFTRA, SAG

STAGE

Wedding Bank	Nelson	Public Theatre
Ain't Suppose to Die a Natural Death	Militant	Broadway
The Basic Training of Pavlo Hummel	Ardell	Public Theatre
The Duplex	Tootsie Franklin (Lead)	Lincoln Center Ballet Theatre
The Dutchman		
Waiting for Godot	Gogo (Tramp)	Nave Theatre

MOTION PICTURES

Willie Dynamite	Pointer	N.Y.
Shamus	Sgt. Dumas	N.Y.
Cotton Comes to Harlem	Detective	N.Y.

TELEVISION

If you give a dance, you got to pay the bank	T-Bone	ABC special
Search for Tomorrow	(cop)	N.Y.

SKILLS

Pantomime, singing, cycling, various athletic abilities

ANN HOWE

Actress, Singer
AEA, AFTRA, AGMA, SAG

300 West 40th Street   Height: 5'4"
New York, New York 10036   Weight: 107
Service: JU 2–4240   Hair: Reddish
                                                Eyes: Brown

EXPERIENCE

BROADWAY   Lost in the Stars w/Brock Peters
                Hello Dolly w/Carol Channing & Ginger Rogers
                   as Mrs. Rose
                Bye Bye Birdie . . . . as Mayor's Wife
                Redhead w/Gwen Verdon

TOURING   Candide—Martin Green, Mary Costa
                Broadway U S A—review—Europe
                Little Mary Sunshine—Nancy Twinkle
                Hello Dolly w/Martha Raye in Viet Nam

STOCK   The Contrast . . . . Letitia
                Song of Norway . . . . . . Nina w/Bill Hayes
                Boys from Syracuse . . . Luciana
                Bye Bye Birdie . . . . Mrs. Macafee
                Little Mary Sunshine . . . Nancy Twinkle
                Guys and Dolls . . . . Sarah Brown
                                             Gordon MacRae
                Carousel . . . . Julie Jordan
                Paint Your Wagon . . . . . Elizabeth w/Allan Jones

OFF BROADWAY   Sweeney Agonistes . . . . Doris
                Jacques Brel—Village Gate
                Devil and Daniel Webster
                Peace "Goddess Abundance"
                Fashion . . . . Mrs. Tiffany

                                             Commercial and
TELEVISION   NBC Opera   Voice over
                Ed Sullivan—Guest   L ist on request
                "Eternal Light"
                Kraft Music Hall

INDUSTRIALS   Jam Handy   Chevrolet, etc.
                House of Shows   Milliken

SPECIAL TALENTS AND TRAINING: Guitar, Dialects, Hartt Music
   College, R.A.D.A., London, England, Berghof School, Dance. Acting—Warren Robertson; Singing—Keith Davis

JOHN COE

210 W. 100th St.	height: 5'8"
New York, N.Y.	weight: 135
service: LO–4–3250	hair: brown
unions: AEA, SAG, AFTRA	eyes: blue
contact:	voice: high baritone

OFF BROADWAY:
THE PROPOSITION—improvised musical—Mercer Arts Center (dir. Alan Albert)

OFF-OFF BROADWAY:
Ronnie—HOUSE OF BLUE LEAVES—Riverside Church (dir. Alan Beck)
Lammemeier—SPRING'S AWAKENING—Public Theatre (dir. Bob Mandel)
Howard—GIRLS MOST LIKELY TO SUCCEED—Clark Center (dir. Russell Treyz)
Pozzo—WAITING FOR GODOT—Nave Theatre (dir. Paul Schneider)
Wilkins—BABYLON CAPTIVITY—Riverside Church (dir. Isaiah Sheffer)
Norman—SINGLE, DOUBLE, KINGSIZE—Nave Theatre (dir. Mark Gordon)
DAWN and THE SUCCESSORS—Clark Center (dir. Anthony DeVito)

REGIONAL THEATRE:
Great Lakes Shakespeare Festival:
Moth—LOVE'S LABOUR'S LOST (dir. Philip Minor)
Clown—THE WINTER'S TALE
Peter—ROMEO AND JULIET (dir. Lawrence Carra)
Truffaldino—SERVANT OF TWO MASTERS
Cut purse/Cadet—CYRANO DE BERGERAC
Second Soldier—ALL'S WELL THAT ENDS WELL
Mike—THE CARETAKER

STOCK: (partial listing of winter, summer, and dinner theatre)

Emcee—CABARET	Allen—PLAY IT AGAIN, SAM
Charlie Brown—CHARLIE BROWN	Norman—STAR-SPANGLED GIRL
George M. Cohan—GEORGE M!	Axel—DON'T DRINK THE WATER
Perchik—FIDDLER ON THE ROOF	Colin—THE KNACK
Dick—DAMES AT SEA	Paul Sevigne—A SHOT IN THE DARK

Hero—FUNNY THING . . .

Billy Jester—LITTLE MARY
              SUNSHINE
Jacquot—CARNIVAL
Mordred—CAMELOT

Jerry, Mike, Richy—LOVERS
AND OTHER STRANGERS

Cass Henderson—ANY
              WEDNESDAY
Renfield—DRACULA

REVUES:
Twist of Lemon—MERRILY OFF THE CUFF—THE REVUE FROM
    HERE

TELEVISION: COMMERCIALS:
Principal Roles: EDGE OF NIGHT   Available on request

TRAINING:
Acting: Jenny Egan, Ted Kazanoff, Peter Feldman
Speech: Robert N. Williams
Voice: Annette Havens, Maurice Jampol
Movement: Bert Stimmel
Musical Theatre: Milton Lyon, Margot Moser
Fencing: Rob Colbin
Dance: Jazz and Tap
Skills: piano, dialects
Denison University (B.A.); Columbia University, School of the Arts
(M.F.A.)

MARY TAFT

Contact: 541—7600   A.E.A., S.A.G., A.F.T.R.A.
                                     HT: 5'7" HAIR: Blnde.
                                     VOICE: Belt

NEW YORK
Plaza 9
    "El Grande de Coca Cola"—Marie
Mercer Arts Center
    "El Grande de Coca Cola" (Drama Desk Award)
    "Playhouse"
Masterworks Laboratory Theatre
    "God of Vengeance"—Hindel
La Mama
    "Dowager's Hump" (dir. Pat Conlon)

Theatre of the Riverside Church
"Babylon Captivity" (dir. Isaiah Sheffer)
Westbeth
"Twelfth Night"—Maria
"Bodies" (Westbeth Feminist Playwrights Collective)
New York Free Theatre (Touring Street Theatre)

REGIONAL
Berkshire Theatre Festival
"Waiting for Godot"—Estragon

DINNER THEATRE
"Tunnel of Love"—Alice Pepper

CHILDREN'S THEATRE
(touring)
"Wizard of Oz"—Cowardly Lion
"Peter Pan"—Nana

COLUMBIA UNIVERSITY SCHOOL OF THE ARTS
"Three Sisters" (dir. Joseph Papp)
"Single, Double, Kingsize" (dir. Mark Gordon)
"The Boyfriend" (dir. Milton Lyon)
"Camino Real" (dir. Carl Weber)
"As You Like It" (dir. Bob Mandel)
"Orestes" (dir. John Dillon)

TELEVISION
"Hell of a Town"

FILM
Documentary: *New York City*

COMMERCIALS
Chase Manhattan Bank
Adolph's Meat Tenderizer
Dr. Atkins Diet Revolution

TRAINING
B.A., College of New Rochelle
M.F.A., Columbia University School of the Arts
Acting: David LeGrant, Warren Robertson Workshop
Voice: Margot Moser, Fred Silver, Jon Peck
Dance: Matt Maddox, Phil Black, Boby Audy

Directing, Teaching, Production Résumés upon Request

PORTFOLIOS

Portfolios are not an immediate essential for actors. You can get through most interviews and auditions with one or two head shots with résumé attached. However, eventually you may want to organize a portfolio, which is an assortment of accumulated professional biographical materials. Portfolios are often useful during initial meetings with advertising agency casting people or agents who want to get a general, overall picture of you and your work.

What goes into a portfolio? You have probably seen a model's portfolio, which is usually a collection of photos— 11" X 14" enlargements, sometimes even larger. Actors don't necessarily have to have such large pictures—often a smaller zipper case fitting 8" X 10"s is used.

Besides the photographs you accumulate—both head and body shots, studio and outdoor and production pictures can be used—keep a file of reviews and programs from shows you do. Anything you can think of that is a visual depiction of something you have done professionally can be included in a portfolio. Keep everything and decide what size portfolio you want to get early on in your career so that you can have photo enlargements made with those proportions in mind (you can always get the enlargement size you want later, but the quality of photographer's originals is usually better than copies.)

When you run into actors with portfolios at interviews or auditions, ask to look at their pictures. This will give you ideas for your own portfolio. When you finally do put together the materials, be creative. Casting people see so many portfolios that any bit of originality done tastefully will catch their eye and may help them remember you.

All these things—pictures, résumé, portfolios—are meant to impress other people, to trigger a positive response to you. So organize a portfolio that will enhance you and contribute to successful interviews.

UNION CARD

At the end of the first chapter I advised you to hold off getting a Union Card until you were ready to work at working professionally full time. Assuming you now have done some non-Equity productions and that you are ready to expand the scope of your audition possibilities, you should begin thinking about getting into Equity.

Why is a union card so important? First of all, you want to work so that you can improve and grow as an actor; secondly, so that you can begin to earn money by your profession. As you get more work, your expanding résumé can create a snowball effect—a working actor with good credits will always have more going for him or her than someone with little experience. The union card is related to all this because, until you have Equity affiliation, you cannot get into a general interview for any Equity shows. Equity shows mean decent salaries, benefits, and working conditions and greater prestige. By this time you may have observed that the trades carry notices for Equity interviews for all kinds of productions. If you go to these interviews and don't have a union card, you won't get past the Equity representative, who is always there, and you won't be seen.

These Equity interviews are not sure tickets to paying jobs. Many Equity members see them as futile exercises. The interviews are required of the producers by Equity law, but often the shows are already cast or the director will only audition actors submitted by agents. However, you have to start somewhere and on occasion a job is gotten through a general interview.

You want to get into an Equity production because then you can get an Equity card. Having an Equity card allows you to get into any Equity interview and, more important, it gives you a psychological boost. You begin to feel that you are indeed a professional actor who is paid for his or her skills.

If you must have an Equity card to get into an Equity interview to get into an Equity production and you can't get an Equity card unless you are in an Equity production, how do you get one? It seems as if Equity doesn't want new members. They don't want anyone to be a member of Equity who isn't good enough to be hired for an Equity show. You must devise some way to get into Equity interviews until you get hired and can get yourself a card.

The situation is not as impossible as it sounds. Often non-Equity people are seen at Equity interviews at the end of the call time or after all the Equity members have been seen. You must ask the Equity representative if you can come back later or wait until the interviewer is free. If you think the interviewer, knowing you are non-Equity, will consider you inexperienced and a risk, you may be right. It's up to you to change his or her mind. Even if you don't get hired, at least you're being seen, and, in this business, personal contact is invaluable. Casting directors have long memories and every time you get through an interview it makes the next one a little easier.

If you use a little ingenuity, you can find ways of arranging auditions for upcoming Equity productions besides crashing an interview. For example, you could find out who is producing a new show and give the office a call or stop by with a picture and résumé and ask if you can see the casting director. Don't go on the same day that they are having Equity interviews because the casting people won't be available. If you want to audition as a replacement for some part in a running show, stop by the theatre and ask for the stage manager, or find out when you can catch him or her with a little free time.

In order to get into your first Equity production you may have to work every angle. Often the normal procedures are just not open to you, so you will have to get out and create your opportunity.

Things can happen almost by accident if you have your antennae out and take advantage of the least opportunity to advance yourself. I got my Equity card and my first Equity job all because of a lucky fluke. I was at an interview for a touring company of a long-running off-Broadway show. The producers had indicated in the trades that they would see both Equity and non-Equity actors. When I got there the theatre was jammed and I signed up as number 200 or so on the non-Equity list. The worst part of the situation was that the interviewers were seeing all the Equity actors first and they numbered in the hundreds. The chances of my being seen before the end of the day were very slim. I was in a showcase production at the time and had a rehearsal scheduled for that afternoon. When I realized I'd never be able to be seen and make it to my rehearsal I decided to leave. Before I took off, however, I hurriedly pushed my way to the ladies' room. As I climbed the stairs leading to the mezzanine where the rest rooms were located, I discovered that the interviews were being held a few feet beyond the ladies' room door. It suddenly occurred to me that on my way out of the rest room I should speak up, tell the interviewers I had to get to a rehearsal and ask them to give me a reading. I had nothing to lose and I might be able at least to get them to take my picture. I did it, and, to shorten the story—they read me right there, I got the job, I got my Equity card, I went on tour with the national company and, unbelievably, ended up in a Broadway revival of the show about six months later. There are many other stories of unexpected good fortune in the business. With the right set of circumstances and a little daring actors can help themselves more than they realize.

Finally, there are other options available to you that are worth mentioning. They are roundabout methods, but no less effective in the long run.

If you are an apprentice for three seasons in an Equity summer-stock theatre, either as a performer or off-stage assistant, you can automatically get an Equity card if the producer decides to hire you under an Equity contract. Working three seasons in any Equity LORT (League of Resident Theatres) production as a nonunion performer or doing three shows within a year in the same Equity dinner theatre as a nonunion performer allows you to join Equity, again at the producer's or director's discretion.

For budgetary reasons many theatres welcome a limited number of non-Equity people. Children's theatres, under Equity contract, audition and hire many non-Equity performers who eventually get their union card this way.

If you work on costumes or with technical crews or even in the office of an Equity production, eventually you may be offered an ASM (assistant stage manager's) contract, which is covered by Equity and automatically gets you into the union.

The first time you work as an extra in a commercial or

television show under the jurisdiction of AFTRA (American Federation of Television and Radio Artists), you may complete the job without joining the union. However, you must join AFTRA before you can accept subsequent extra work, if your second job comes thirty days or more after the first job. Even if you are not too interested in working in television or commercials, remember that one extra job can get you into AFTRA, and membership in AFTRA automatically allows you to join Equity after a six-month wait and SAG (Screen Actors Guild) after a twelve-month wait (if you can prove to SAG that you have had an AFTRA job).

Neither Equity nor SAG can be your parent union (first union you join) unless you can prove that you have been hired for an Equity or SAG production (as a SAG principal). AFTRA, on the other hand, allows you to join without any stipulations, that is, you can join without having an AFTRA job. If you have the spare $300 initiation fee plus $23.75 in dues you can join AFTRA, wait six months, and automatically join Equity for a discount membership fee of $150. However, if the first professional job you get is under an Equity contract, you must pay full Equity dues and Equity then becomes your parent union. If your first job is under AFTRA, then AFTRA remains your parent union and you don't have to pay the full initiation fee to Equity.

To join SAG you must either have proof that you have been hired as a *principal* in a SAG production or prove that you have been a member of AFTRA for twelve months and have had an AFTRA job.

Many actors get their Equity cards by joining AFTRA first. It's a legitimate procedure and, if you don't mind paying two initiation fees as well as two sets of dues, you have assurance of an Equity card.

After the six-month wait you can even go on inactive membership in AFTRA and not have to pay dues. If you're not getting or going after television work, you may as well go inactive—you can activate at any time.

Joining AFTRA so that you can eventually get your Equity card does not mean you can't continue to try and get into an Equity production during the six-month wait. The sooner you get your Equity card the better. Being able to put

Equity on your résumé is extremely helpful. It's not that the union membership itself has inherent value, but it puts you into another class. Sometimes the non-Equity label is too glaring in the eyes of casting people. While they may not pay you respect just because they notice you are an Equity member, they often will not bother to give you any attention at all when they see only non-Equity credits. A union card doesn't have to have top priority in assembling your actor's kit, but it has its place and its importance in your career. (See Chapter 6 for complete explanation of the three actors' unions.)

ANSWERING SERVICES

There is not too much to explain about the necessity of an answering service. You must have some way of getting calls when you are not reachable at home. Every actor has nightmares about having a successful audition and not getting the job because the message didn't get through in time.

There are several kinds of answering services available in New York with varying special features and degrees of reliability. Many services advertise in the trades and range in cost from five dollars to fifteen dollars per month.

Before choosing a service, ask several other actors for their suggestions. You will probably hear three or four of the more popular services named most often. It's usually a safe bet to go with a widely used service.

Most services will either try to reach you as soon as a message comes in (sometimes at added cost) or simply take the messages and give them to you when you call in.

Not all services operate twenty-four hours a day and some are just not as accommodating as others. You can't really know what to expect from services unless you talk to people who already use them. Some actors will rave about their service because the operators are friendly or the service has gotten them auditions or work. Some services do help their clients in this way because they often are called by producers or agencies looking for actors. At any rate, take time to investigate the services. Get plenty of feedback from other actors and make your decision with the realization that changing services, after you have left your service number with several agents and interviewers and perhaps had the number printed on your pictures, is an expensive and troublesome ordeal.

You might want to look into home answering devices. These attach to your phone and allow callers to record messages for you when you are out. Some of these devices allow you to call into them from outside to pick up your messages. The prices vary according to quality and complexity. You can expect to pay from around $100 to $500.

Once you begin going to interviews and auditions and passing out pictures and résumés, don't delay getting a service. Sometimes the nightmare of missing out on a job because of a phone mix-up becomes a reality. Even to miss out on an audition or call-back because you couldn't be reached is an incalculable loss. Avoid the risk of these horrors and get yourself an answering service immediately.

PERSONAL APPEARANCE AND ATTITUDE

There's one other thing you have to put in order along with your pictures, résumé, union affiliation, and answering service—that's you. How you look and behave at interviews and auditions is just about as important as how well you read for the role.

An interviewer collects your picture, he looks through your résumé, but what he's most interested in is what you look like in person, your manner, even sometimes how you talk. Don't panic—you don't have to start from scratch and redo your face or your personality. But you must be sure that you know what you have going for you: how well you can look, how interesting you can be, how together you can seem, even how good an actor or actress you are. Knowing all this about yourself is the first step; developing and using these things is the next part of the game plan.

There's the real real you, a multiemotional person with or without hang-ups, feeling good some days and terrible on others. Then there's the real you that you take with you into every interview and audition, always looking well and seeming pleasant and unhassled, capable and self-possessed, even when the real real you may feel otherwise. While interviewers and directors are put off by pretense, self-conscious flamboyance, "kookiness," or obvious role-playing in actors (unless, of course, that's what the part you're up for demands), they are equally turned off by someone who walks in with their vulnerabilities or bad moods or insecurities or personal problems showing. They don't want phonies. They want the real professional you, but—and always keep this distinction in mind—not the real personal you. Leave that side of you at home or keep it covered up (*protected* is a better word) by your professional persona.

The deep emotions and intimate facts of your personality may be helpful on stage in the creation of a part, but they don't really have any place in an interview. Casting officials just don't want to be troubled or embarrassed by total honesty.

The greatest advantage in the development of this aura, this "professional persona," is that it is a protection device, a guard plate against the rejections, the rudeness, the insensitivity, the flesh-peddling part of the business. It's difficult to cope with rejections, which are part of every actor's professional life, and the inhumanity of some of the people you have to deal with—directors or producers or agents or other actors. If you can let your professional persona act as a buffer and deal with the ugly side of the business, you can save your real self a lot of misery.

There is no way of keeping some of those rejections from breaking through and affecting the real real you—otherwise you wouldn't be human. But since the rejections have nothing to do with you as a person and concern you only as a professional actor, try to keep them in this perspective and don't let them intrude upon your personal life. If you try to understand and develop this distinction between the personal you and the professional you early in your career, your chances of enduring and having a successful professional life and a stable personal life are much greater.

If you can see the whole interview—judgment—rejection or acceptance part of the business as a kind of game, nonthreatening and not entirely serious, it will be easier for you to create your professional persona, as if you were always going to a costume party or playing at "pretend" as children do, in earnest and spontaneously, with imagination and a certain bravado.

When you go to any interview or audition, say something by your appearance. Strive for definition rather then vagueness; try to be distinct without being obtrusive. First of all, you want to look well put together. So choose your clothes, hairstyle, accessories (women, choose your makeup) with care and some sense of cohesiveness. Whether you want to look casual or dressy, be stylish and tasteful about it. If you can, add a little flair to your look—something that catches the eye and subtly, *subtly* distinguishes you.

If you are going to an interview or audition for a specific role or play, try to accentuate your closeness to the character or mood of the show by your appearance. For instance if you are a young person going to an audition for *Moonchildren*, a play about a group of college students, don't dress like a businessman or a high-fashion model. Look at the cast breakdown of any play in the trades—usually there is a brief description of each role—and let your appearance fit into the style of the character closest to you. If you are going for a commercial audition, ask your agent what sort of person you're supposed to be. If it's a clergyman or a gas-station attendant, be sure to dress to harmonize rather than distract.

Give the interviewer, the director, or the casting person what is wanted—someone whose look reminds them of or in some way links up with one of the characters. Don't be too obvious. You don't have to look exactly like a cheap hussy or a Bowery wino, but only like someone who could easily make the transition.

One of my first auditions was for the part of a Hell's Angel's girl friend. I thought I would dress the part exactly, so I went in wearing sleek pants and black turtleneck with a neck chain, a man's leather motorcycle jacket and a helmet. Not only did I feel foolish and uncomfortable, but I probably looked ridiculous. Sensing that, I left my jacket and helmet in the outer room and discovered that the pants and turtleneck were quite enough to give me the appropriate "feel" for the lines and the interviewer a sense of my ability to resemble the girl in the film. I liked the way I looked in the pants and top and realized in time that the jacket and helmet were unnecessary and amateurish. Let my lesson serve you as well: Dress to feel attractive and comfortable and distinctive and try to approximate the style of the character without being heavy-handed or sacrificing good taste.

If you want to play this game well, then just getting your appearance together is not enough. The way you "perform" as yourself in an interview is the important complement to how you look.

The ideal way to behave is as yourself when you feel terrific—self-confident, gregarious, relaxed—at your best. Unfortunately, interviews and auditions are not spontaneous meetings of good friends but forced and arbitrary confrontations of strangers sizing up each other.

If you happen to be in a poor frame of mind—nervous, worried about the impression you're making, desperate to get a job, generally depressed—being totally yourself is not going to do you much good. You have to find some way to "psych" yourself, to turn a potentially nerve-jangling, uncomfortable interview into a pleasant and relaxed experience.

Some actors see interviews as a challenge, a clash of wills, with the aggressor the winner. Others have such a devil-may-care, cynical attitude that you sometimes wonder why they bothered to come in the first place. The hazards of these two extremes should be obvious. You'd be surprised at the hundreds of misguided actors who have settled on one or the other of them as their way of coping with interviews.

Other methods actors sometimes use are the cajole, "leave them paralyzed with laughter" approach, or the freak-out, "shock them out of their indifference." Who can say if either of these approaches has a chance for success? If you are by nature a comic or a weirdo, you might be able to pull them off. What works for you is what works. When you start getting feedback, positive response from interviews, then you must be on the right track. You may not be called back for every interview or signed up on the spot. There are some variables over which you have no control that will keep you from certain jobs: age, coloring, height, weight, and so on.

But if your instincts tell you that the interview went well, that the person enjoyed talking to you, that you made some kind of direct contact with him or her, then you should credit yourself with a success. It's like any other human situation. Interviewers may be as tense, insecure, and tired (underneath their interviewer's facade) as you. If you can put them at ease and send out positive, open, friendly vibrations, you can relieve some of the pressure of the situation and usually get a favorable response.

A casting director for a New York production company, when asked what makes her remember or eliminate actors she meets at general interviews, told two instructive stories. On one occasion she had taken a break from the interviews and gone to the ladies' room. As she went to the basin to wash up, a young woman applying the finishing touches to her makeup refused to make room for her. "Can't you see I'm in a hurry? I have an important interview in a few minutes." You can imagine the shock and horror awaiting this actress when she discovered her interviewer was the person she had rebuffed in the lavatory. The lesson of this incident, according to the casting director, is that actors should realize they often are judged even before they walk into the interview. She says that many times she has asked the receptionist's reaction to a particular actor as he or she waited to be interviewed.

She followed up with a story of an actor who walked into his interview late in the day with a cup of coffee. He offered it to her and said something like "This is for you because it's late and you must be tired, and, besides, I want you to remember me." She said that very few actors are ever that considerate of the interviewer, and this actor's honesty about his "other" motive was as appreciated as the coffee.

Learn to leave your fear and tension and insecurity at home and take to all interviews a confident, relaxed, outgoing you. This is the essence of the professional persona: you at your best even when underneath you feel otherwise.

Now you have some idea of what makes up an actor's equipment: the pictures, résumé, union card, answering service, and the professional persona. The first four items are easy enough to acquire, when the money is available. The last is something that will come in time simply by your working at it. It's not easy to achieve this elusive "aura." It is a unique discovery for each actor. It's like learning how to swim. You'll have to go under a few times, flail around a bit, and learn to allay your fears and relax before you can move confidently through the water, before the technique you bring to interviews and auditions becomes an unconscious skill.

CHAPTER 4

Making Contact

Getting your equipment together is the first priority. You're now ready to put that equipment to use, to get out there and make contact, again and again and again. Getting to know agents and casting directors, passing out your picture at interviews, and making the rounds can be boring and tiresome, sometimes humiliating and frustrating. Why is it so important to keep yourself continually in circulation? The more you meet people in a position to help you and get their attention and interest, the more proficient you become at the necessary, less pleasant side of the acting business: getting the audition that gets you the job that finally allows you to act. Your employment will be directly influenced by how hard you work to get it.

Certainly you can't sit back and wait for auditions to come your way, and neither can you always be satisfied with following normal channels. Going to Equity interviews often leads nowhere. You'll have to find other ways of making contact with the producers, directors, and casting people and getting them to audition you. In other words, if there isn't an obvious direct route to a job available, you have to make your own opening, create your own set of favorable circumstances.

How far beyond "normal procedure" can you go? You are limited only by the bounds of good taste. As long as you don't invite censure by unprofessional behavior, by pushing yourself into an inappropriate situation, or doing something annoying, embarrassing, or rude, you risk nothing but a rejection. Using sex to get a job is a mistake. It might work once or twice but mixing work and personal life is a dangerous risk. Theatre gossip is virulent and deadly. Besides, there are too many good actors around who can win jobs strictly on the merits of their acting ability.

EQUITY INTERVIEWS

Going to Equity interviews has certain advantages. First, you may be one of the lucky ones who gets called back to audition. Second, you get a chance to meet the casting person or director or producer who takes your picture, and third, you are in the midst of other actors who talk about the business—their auditions, jobs, acting or voice teachers, another interview to go to. You may pick up some useful information.

Also, you get yourself into the "making contact" cycle. In the early stages of your career the interviews give you a helpful head start in establishing a routine. Most of the arranging has been done ahead of time. The only effort you have to make is to read the trades or the bulletin board at Equity, find out where and when the interviews are being held, go on the appointed day with your Equity card, show it to the Equity representative, sign the list, and wait for your turn.

Attendance at interviews varies with the seasons. Usually New York productions attract large numbers during the fall and winter. During the spring when summer-stock auditions are held, interviews for out-of-town productions also become very popular. The summer months are usually slow; few interviews are held and not too many actors are around for them.

If you know a show has popular appeal, go early, if possible an hour or so before the interviews are scheduled to begin, and get your name on the upper portion of the list. Early in the day, casting people are fresh and alert. As the day wears on, the latecomer risks meeting a tired, hungry, and restless interviewer.

If you have other things to do during the day and you have quite a wait for your turn, you can sign the list, leave, and return close to when your number comes up. Mention to the Equity representative that you'd like to leave and he or she will tell you whether or not you can expect to be squeezed in if your number is passed. Usually there is no problem, but some representatives feel that other actors are inconvenienced by latecomers and they won't accommodate them.

The interview itself usually lasts between two and ten minutes, depending on the interviewer's efficiency or interest. Five minutes may not seem like a very long time to you but the usually large number of people necessitates speedy turnover, and, after all, the interview is not an audition but a process of elimination and selection for later readings. As noted earlier, the interviewer may only be a collector of pictures and résumés who makes no decisions but only gives over his accumulated pile to the director.

If the decision is made at the interview itself, it will be done relatively quickly and you may or may not be told. Sometimes the interviewer, if he or she wants to have you come in for an audition, will set up an appointment for you right there. Often you will be told on the spot that you aren't right for anything in the show and even offered back your picture. Consider this a favor. At least you aren't left hanging and, since pictures are expensive, you may as well rescue it from the wastebasket and keep it for the next interview.

Being typed out happens so frequently that you'll come to accept it as a normal procedure. You can help the situation by being sure you read the cast breakdown carefully and honestly assess if you do or don't fit the description of one of the characters. You may know that you can play a particular part beautifully, and if you want to try and convince the interviewer of that, go ahead. But interviewers don't always have a stretchable imagination; they only know that you do or don't look the part.

Most frequently no commitment is made one way or the other at the interview. If you are going to be called back it will usually be within the next few days, unless the interviewer mentions there is to be a delay. You can always ask when they plan to have call-backs. Questions are okay but avoid anything that seems as if you are trying to pin down the interviewer. He or she isn't going to tell you much more than general information and may resent your asking for anything more.

Equity interviews, "cattle calls" as they often are called, have a negative side as well. You sometimes have to wait hours, literally, to be seen. The waste of time and energy can be enormous. But you will begin to realize why it is so important to move beyond the limited opportunities of Equity interviews. If this is the only benefit you get from them, that they encourage you to find other ways of getting auditions, the Equity interviews have served a useful purpose.

MAKING THE ROUNDS

One effective way of making contact is "making the rounds." To do this well you should approach it in an efficient, organized way—make a project out of it. Before you even get started, make a commitment to keep at it zealously until you start getting feedback.

Making the rounds does not mean going around and visiting every agent, production house, and casting director in town once and then you're finished. If that was all it took to make rounds successfully, actors would be ecstatic. Making the initial contact is easy compared to the follow-up, which is finding a way of mushrooming the first meeting into a professional relationship and establishing several trunk lines between you and agents, production companies, and casting directors.

Making the rounds can be less of an ordeal if you know about and use some basic tools. The first is the Ross Report, a small pamphlet published by Television Index, Inc., that lists just about every advertising agency, casting director, agent, television studio, New York television program, and producer and commercial producer. The Ross Report can be purchased for $1.25 at 150 Fifth Avenue or the AFTRA New York Local office at 1350 Avenue of the Americas. Since the Ross Report is published at monthly intervals, you are assured of an up-to-date listing with corrected names, addresses, and phone numbers. There are over two hundred fifty listings in the Ross Report, more than enough to keep you busy for several months.

Another essential tool is a combination daily appointment book/telephone and address directory. Get one that will fit into a portfolio or purse or coat pocket so that it's handy at all times. You'll need a reliable reminder of appointments and auditions and telephone contacts and an orderly address book for immediate reference. Three-quarters of successful rounds-making is that you establish a well-organized, regular routine. You may want to keep a chart such as the one given below to keep a record of your progress. It is important to keep track of initial appointment dates and frequency of subsequent contacts. You shouldn't let too much time elapse between visits or calls or postcards, but you should also be careful not to overexpose yourself. The idea is to remind, not to pester. Get all these items before you start making the rounds so that you are well organized even before your first appointment.

For the appointment itself, you of course must have a supply of pictures and résumés. A portfolio is not essential, but it would certainly be a useful addition at this point and an impressive way to introduce yourself at the first appointment with any office.

After you have been to an office once you may want to keep in touch with postcards between visits and phone calls. Often an agent or casting director will say that he or she resents being called every week but likes to receive postcards. Your photo reproduction office is the place to go for picture postcards. Choose your favorite 8" X 10" and get yourself a

SAMPLE "ROUNDS" CHART

AGENT	AGENCY	DATES SEEN	POSTCARDS	TELEPHONE	COMMENTS
Ruth Grant	Brown & Baxter	8/9	8/13 8/27 9/5 9/24 10/3	9/26 10/10	Frequent postcards
Joan Rogers	Creativity, Inc	8/14	9/5 9/24 10/13 10/16 10/26	10/9	Postcards; new pix
Jane Best	Jane Best	6/5	7/23 9/24 10/3 10/26	10/9	Postcards; commercials
Mack First	Mack First Agency	8/7 10/10	8/13 8/27 9/24 10/3 10/16	9/26 10/24	Keep after; new pix
Tom Williams	Alice Topping	7/26 9/26	8/7 8/13 8/27 9/5		Commercials; audition 7/26
Martin Sawyer	Michael Ray	8/29 10/25	9/5 9/24 10/3 10/16		Postcards; pictures

number of postcard-size reproductions. Prices range from twenty dollars to thirty dollars for two hundred cards. The back is usually left blank for your written note, the address, and a stamp. Be sure to have your name and answering-service number printed on the same side as the picture. This is an effective, relatively painless way of keeping in touch with offices, when you don't want to call or visit for a few weeks.

Now that you know all the tools you need for making the rounds, how do you go about putting them to use? Getting in to see agents, casting directors, advertising agency casting personnel, and production companies is not always easy. Neither is it always impossible. In some instances you may reach a dead end, but since there are so many other doors to try, you needn't worry.

First you must decide what sort of work you are interested in getting. The Ross Report, as you will see, lists all franchised agents, but it doesn't specify which area each agent handles. (Since the Ross Report is a television reference, all the agencies listed submit for TV shows, but most of them cover other media.) Some only submit actors for commercials, some for stage and film work as well, some only for television and films. Some large agencies, and even a few small operations, do everything.

If you are looking for work in all areas, you won't have to bother with finding out which agencies are specialized. But if you are not interested in every field, you should find out ahead of time which agencies would be useless to you. One easy way is to call the office—anonymously or not—and ask if they submit in all areas or only in specific ones.

The same is true of the independent casting directors listed in the Ross Report. You may want to do a little investigating before you try to get an appointment with them. Some do only commercials and films, some also handle stage productions.

Obviously the separate listing of television studios and shows with the names of their own casting directors speaks for itself. The advertising agencies listed in the Ross Report cast for commercials and soap operas generally. Some do only commercials.

Some agencies and casting directors hold open-interview hours once a week or even daily. Find out which offices do so, either from other actors, the Equity bulletin board, or by calling the offices and asking. You may find a large number of actors waiting, and it will remind you of an open Equity call. Whether these open-interview hours are effective is a decision you'll have to make. Certainly it's worth trying, and, if you get positive feedback, go back the following week. If you make several return visits without getting any action from the agent or casting director, you may be wasting time. It's difficult to know sometimes if the person behind the desk is truly interested and would submit you when something comes up or if they are only going through the motions of empty cordiality. One way of finding out if they are willing to work for you is to ask them on one of your return visits (not too soon) if they would submit you for a specific production or show that you know is currently casting. Tell them which part you want to be submitted for and the other details. Usually the response you get will be a real indication of their attitude toward you. If they get the audition for you—great. If not, it's up to you to decide if it's worth while keeping after them.

Usually it is better to make an appointment with someone in an office instead of just dropping by unannounced. Many agencies have a sign on the door saying "By appointment only." This sign should be respected if you are a total stranger to the office. Some doors are kept locked and you'll be told to slip your picture under the door. If you can find a way of getting an appointment with such an office you have a much better chance of getting their attention than if you simply slip your picture under the door or hand it to a receptionist.

An ideal way of making an appointment for an initial meeting is by referral. If you can get permission to use the name of a friend or teacher or fellow actor who is in professional or personal contact with an agent or casting person, you have a much better chance of getting an appointment. Simply by saying, "So-and-so suggested I call and arrange an appointment with you," you increase the likelihood of a positive response—if, of course, your reference is a legitimate one. Most people won't tell you to use their names unless they know it will mean something. Once you get the appointment you are on your own. The referral can get you inside the door, but don't count on it getting you more. You have to take over once the appointment is made.

Another way of getting in for an appointment is by using your acting work. If you are in a showcase or a show on or off Broadway, try to get as many agents and casting people as possible to come see it. Call various offices and ask if you can arrange for tickets; if possible, get the exact date when the agent or casting person plans to come. Usually you can expect a good response for any legitimate production—agents and casting people spend a good deal of time going to the theatre looking for talent. They don't always like to go to showcases, but if they have a free night and the theatre isn't too out of the way and if you call the day before or the morning of the performance to remind them, they might come.

When you are in a showcase and have a large enough part or a good cameo appearance and you are pleased with your work, get a stack of flyers from whoever is in charge of them. Even low-budget showcases usually have flyers. If not, make your own announcements and mail them to as many offices as you can. Follow up in a few days with a call and ask if they got the flyer, and if anyone in the office would like to come, and could you make reservations. Chances are no one will make an immediate commitment, but if they show any interest, call again shortly before or during the run and remind them.

You may get calls from agents and casting personnel who see you in a show and want to meet you. This is the most gratifying way of getting an appointment. Many times, however, you have to follow up on people you think saw you perform. Call a day or so later, identify yourself and the show and ask if you can come in for an appointment. If the person is someone you had spoken to before and if they didn't come, they may give you an appointment anyway— half out of guilt. If the person says, yes, they saw you, and no, they can't arrange an appointment at this time, don't lose heart. The refusal may have nothing to do with how well or poorly you performed. If you are a type that the office doesn't use or if they already have a number of signed clients of your quality, they may not need you at that time.

Often you go through all the work of mailing flyers and phoning and phoning again and get only one person to come. But that is enough to make it all worth your time. That one person may start calling you for work or remember you later when something comes up for your type. They may even recommend you to someone else. Even if you don't get immediate replies, getting people to come and see you can have long-range benefits.

The other way of getting appointments without any reference or acting work to help is the "hard labor" method. This takes time and persistence and patience. You can begin by calling an office outright and asking for an appointment. Almost always the response is "Send us a picture and résumé first." Before you hang up, ask who in the office is handling whatever you're most interested in, such as theatre or commercials. (Some agencies have different people working different fields.) *Get a name* whenever possible because then you can address your picture and résumé to a specific person in the office. On your follow-up call, ask to speak directly to that person. Phones are answered by receptionists, usually, who may or may not be accommodating. Often half the battle is learning how to get beyond the secretaries. When you do get to speak to someone in the inner office, use your charm, your enthusiasm, your charisma, whatever it takes to get them interested. Remember, though, that many times you won't get beyond the receptionist or secretary, so you will have to keep calling office after office until you do. Usually his or her function is to pacify callers with false promises of return calls or out-to-lunch excuses, and the like. Receptionists don't discriminate among strangers; usually everyone is a nusiance to them, even if their phone voices belie it. Often appointments are gotten because the secretary is out of the office for a few minutes and the boss answers the phone. Capitalize on every opportunity.

Not all receptionists have to be stumbling blocks. Some can be helpful, and often they have more influence in an office than you might think, especially if the agency is small. In that case the receptionist may be on double duty, answering phones and helping with casting. Be sure you treat the receptionist with the same deference and respect that you would pay the head person. For all you know, he or she may be the head person. Everyone wants to feel important, and receptionists should respond favorably and be kindly disposed toward you if you don't slight them or belittle their position.

When you do start getting appointments, be careful not to schedule them too close together. Leave enough time between appointments on the same day to allow for long waits and traveling from office to office. By now, if you have been to open calls or any open-hour interviews with agents or casting personnel, you know what to expect at appointments. Often your résumé is a conversation focus. Sometimes the interviewer tells you what areas the office handles and/or asks what kind of work interests you.

The interviewer may ask if you are willing to do extra work—nonspeaking walk-ons in soap operas or background in commercials and films. Usually you can't lose anything by saying yes. Only actors who have done a great deal of principal work in television and commercials shy away from extra work: first, because they probably don't need the money, and second, because it's a prestige loss. However, if you are at the beginning stages of your career, don't be afraid to take extra work. Doing so does not label you as "only extra material" unless you choose to limit yourself to that. In fact, being an extra can be an extremely useful and instructive experience. You can be unobtrusive while learning about what goes on in a television studio or at a film or commercial shoot. Extra work is not very demanding on your acting skills, so you don't have to worry too much about that. Besides, the money is pretty good and you are making excellent professional contacts with directors, producers, and so on.

At some appointments you may be asked to read for the interviewer. He or she may want to get a general idea of your quality and range and acting ability. Or, if you are lucky enough to hit an office at the right time you may be asked to read for something currently being cast. Put this out of your mind before any appointment because it happens only rarely. Besides, it does no good to build up anxiety over the possibility that you may be asked to read, even if you are.

If you have any questions for the interviewer that aren't automatically answered during the conversation, ask them. Find out how they like actors to keep in touch—phone calls, return visits, postcards—and make a note of their preference. Of course, if you are currently in a show, ask if you can arrange for tickets. If you have a commercial that is currently running on television or radio, mention it.

The conversation doesn't have to be a one-sided exchange with you only answering when spoken to. You may want to ask advice or introduce a relevant topic. Try not to listen to yourself and weigh every word you utter. Nothing you say is so momentous that it could put your career in jeopardy. Be as spontaneous and loose as possible and forget about what effect your comments are having. Most casting people don't recall the exact words of a conversation but they do remember the manner of the actor and whether or not they enjoyed the meeting.

When the interviewer begins to bring the appointment to a close, gracefully take the hint and get ready to leave. If the interviewer hasn't already asked for a picture and résumé for the files, be sure to offer them.

As you leave, don't worry about whether or not you made a good impression. Just decide if the exchange offers promise of future feedback. If you can't tell one way or the other, keep the agent or casting person on your list for rounds-making and keeping in touch. Only eliminate people who come right out and tell you they can't do anything for you or who seem to have very little interest in seeing or hearing from you again.

Remember that the success of making the rounds depends on how industriously you pursue a contact and how you nurture and attend the seeds of the first appointment. Unless the meeting is a definite write-off, enter all contacts on your chart and let your later efforts at developing the relationship determine whether or not you get feedback.

In making the rounds you may have a negative, humiliating experience or two. If an agent or casting director or any professional contact rubs you the wrong way or vice versa, don't lash out, don't try to get even or put them in their place. It's not worth exciting yourself. Remember, this isn't the real world. You may make an enemy when you could just as easily settle for passing out of their heads.

You're not always going to get the respect and kindness you deserve. That is the nature of the game. You are the one looking for work and *they* are the ones who pass it out. Sometimes this illusory sense of power over actors feeds the insecurities of some agents or producers or casting people and they can be plain nasty. When you come up against this, be cool. You needn't back out with your tail between your legs, but don't mistakenly assume you gain anything by returning the nastiness and really making a name for yourself.

There are some awful people in the business and you're bound to run into a few of them as you go from office to office. Knowing about it ahead of time may help you to deal with it when and if it comes up. The majority of agents, producers, and casting directors more than make up for the few rotten eggs. But you know how rotten eggs can smell up the whole basket. The point is, don't let any bad incident disrupt your routine or put you off making the rounds altogether. Just hold your breath until you get out the door and walk on to the next office.

There are several reasons that making the rounds is worth the investment of your time and energy. The first immediate advantage is that your picture and résumé get into the general files of casting offices, agents, producers. This in itself may someday get you a call for work or an audition. When agents or casting people look for actors to submit, they usually first go to their active files. These consist either of their signed clients or of people they have sent up for auditions frequently on a free-lance basis. They may have seen an actor perform recently and decided to put him or her on the active list. If by chance they don't find the type they need on their active sheet, they may turn to the general files and thumb through the hundreds of pictures of all the people who have dropped by—maybe just once—in order to find an actor to submit. This explains why actors sometimes get a call from an office that they visited a year or two earlier and never heard from or got in touch with since. This happens infrequently and it's not a very reliable way of getting auditions. But by getting yourself inside the door and into the general files, you have at least made a tiny opening for yourself, and if you can capitalize on the initial meeting, you may be able to get into the active files.

A long-range advantage resulting from making the rounds is that you get to know various agents and casting people and they get to know you. In theatre, familiarity breeds respect.

Somehow a known quantity is much more appealing to an agent, producer, or casting person than an unknown. Almost always, if there is a choice to be made between a familiar face and a stranger, the familiar face wins out.

Often agents or casting people like your look or have seen your work and want to submit you when something comes along that you're right for. If they have a recent enough recollection of you, then chances are you'll get submitted. That's why repeated visits or contacts, especially to people who initially give you a positive response, are so important. One day you'll hit them at the right time and they'll have something for you. But you have to remind them of your face frequently enough so that they'll remember to call you. Many casting people say that they often draw blanks when it comes to finding actors to submit. Probably because they see so many faces, the ones they set apart for later calls get lost in the jumble. You have to become like a flashing light in the heads of agents and casting people.

Almost always you can expect to advance your career by making the rounds, if—and this bears repeating—you conscientiously establish and rigorously follow your personal "rounds" routine and if you commit yourself to staying with it for at least a year. It may take six months before you even get one call to audition, but that first call usually signals a bigger payoff to come. For one thing, it boosts your morale. You know the effort you made had effect. So you go at the rounds with renewed enthusiasm. And when you get a job as a result of making the rounds, an even greater snowball effect takes place. The more industriously you make rounds the more you increase the chances of your getting auditions, and, obviously, the more auditions you get the greater the odds of your getting work.

AGENTS

How important is having an agent? Are the actors with agents really better off? Do they get all the work and make all the money? If you get an agent, will all your problems be solved, is that the key to a successful acting career? How do you know who the "good" agents are? How do you get an agent?

Agents have two main functions: they search out and arrange auditions for actors and they negotiate contracts for jobs won by their clients. Agents are middlemen not just for actors, but for directors and producers as well who can't and don't want to see every actor in town for their shows. They trust that agents have separated the wheat from the chaff for them. Agent-submitted actors, whether or not they deserve it, have the reputation of being more reliable, more talented, even—if it matters—more prestigious, because the agent says so.

Do agents deserve this kind of power? Deserve or not, in a business full of many people who don't belong, a sifting out process is necessary. But agents don't have a corner on the market. In fact, some good working actors don't want to use and feel they don't need agents. But even they will concede that most film, commercial, and television work and a large percentage of legitimate jobs are gotten by agent-submitted actors. Of course there are exceptions. Extra work is not usually handled through agents, and, in some unusual situations, actors may get a reading for a principal part in a film or television show on their own. But very few commercial auditions are handled except through agents or casting directors or by recommendation. Sometimes the advertising agency's own casting director will call actors directly, but, for the most part, he or she prefers to work through agents. This, by the way, is why making the rounds of agents and freelance casting directors should take priority over visits to advertising agencies and television casting personnel, if you are interested in more than extra work.

The non-agent-represented actor still has a fighting chance of getting auditions for legitimate stage productions. Even though many Broadway, Off-Broadway, and out-of-town shows ask agents for submissions—even some showcases are cast through agents—they often audition nonagent actors as well. Open interviews are held for almost every legitimate show. However, as you well know, open interviews often are meaningless because the show is already cast or the producers have already lined up auditions for agent-submitted actors.

Your career is not destined to fail if you don't have an agent. You can struggle along and eventually get some auditions on your own. Neither is success guaranteed if you do get an agent to work for you. You still have to beat out all the competition to win the job. But getting the audition is sometimes as difficult, if not more so, than getting the job. If agents are not essential, they are certainly a very big help.

There are three kinds of agencies: large, established institutions employing hundreds of agents; smaller, respected offices employing a handful of agents, usually still run by the person who started the agency, and very small sometimes reliable operations who handle a small number of clients and have only one or two people in the office. The first two types of agencies have a proven track record. They have been and will be around for a long time. In the last category fall many of the "fly-by-night" operations that go nowhere except out of business in a fairly short time.

When choosing which agencies to cover as you make rounds, you can usually rely on shop talk. Active and hustling agents make a fast name for themselves among actors. Ask actors you meet at auditions who submits them. You'll hear some names over and over again. Often you may find a very small, new agency more willing to meet you because they are still in the market for clients. Older agencies often don't even bother interviewing new actors. They are content to handle only their signed clients or free-lance actors who have been submitted by them often in the past.

When you begin getting calls from various agents you can expect to hear from them again if you have a good audition. A good audition means either that you get the job or you get one or more call-backs. Don't expect, by the way, that agents necessarily will ask you to sign as one of their contracted talents. Many agents and actors prefer to free-lance with one another. This is usually to your advantage, especially if several agents are submitting you. When you sign with one agent, you often can be submitted only by him or her. Early in your career this can be very limiting unless the agent you sign with devotes a great deal of time to you. It's always a safe bet to free-lance for a while until you build up a permanent working relationship and rapport with one particular agency.

When you do get a job through an agent—free-lance or not—he or she will negotiate for your salary and the terms of the contract. An agent currently is allowed a 10 percent commission in AFTRA and SAG contracts and a 5 or 10 percent commission in Equity contracts. Usually the agent will get you enough above scale wage to cover the 5 or 10 percent. If you have any difficulties with money or working conditions, tell your agent, who will serve as a middleman. A good agent will fight for your rights and protect your interests.

When you get good results from an agent, you become a valuable commodity. You may discover that his or her attitude toward you changes radically from casual interest to extreme friendliness. This sudden attention may be fleeting—business is business, remember. At any rate, it would be unwise to overestimate your "in-ness" with any agent. They have many other clients and sometimes very limited attention spans. Don't expect that you can ever know what an agent is really like or how much he or she likes you. If you get a job, you are of course more "popular" in the office. Agents are first and foremost in the business of talent-pushing. As long as you deal with them on this level—in an amicable business relationship—you should be able to keep the agent game in perspective. You may still have to keep up the "remind" routine, even though you have gotten a job through an agency. Even as a signed client you may be neglected unless you keep after your agent with occasional visits and phone calls. Many actors check in regularly, every day or so, with agents who submit them. The frequency of your calls should be based on the feedback you are getting. If an agent says, "Nothing now, talk to you next week," or "I may have something tomorrow, call me," just accept that and respond accordingly.

A few words on the protocol of agent submission. As was mentioned, when you get a job through an agent, he or she expects to handle all the negotiating. Whenever any question arises with a producer over money or work hours or transportation arrangements, or the like, take it to the agent. Not only does he or she get paid for this kind of service, but you may overstep your place if you try to handle what is considered the agent's job.

When any audition is arranged for you by an agent—even someone you may never have met—you must present yourself at the audition as sent up by that agent. If the producer should ask how to contact you, give the agent's number. If you should be called back and the information is not passed on through your agent, always let him or her know immediately. Otherwise you could unwittingly cheat the agent out of a commission and that is a bad move. Whatever audition you get on your own is yours, but anytime an agent submits you, even at your suggestion, you must deal through him or her. Cheating an agent, consciously or not, can have disastrous consequences. You can be blackballed or bad-mouthed or worse. Just don't do it.

Before you sign with any agent, be sure that he or she is franchised by the unions. Look at the most recent edition of the Ross Report and, if the agent doesn't appear on the list, call AFTRA or Equity and ask the agent department if the agent has been franchised. If not, be very wary of signing any contract. The unions have spent years trying to set up a protection system for actors in their dealings with agents. However, they have no authority to intercede for you if you should have problems with an agent who is not franchised by them. Any signed contract, union or nonunion, is a binding legal document, and any agent who uses other than standard union contracts is a questionable ally. He or she can legally entangle you in a one-sided (their side) agreement, the full repercussions of which you may not even be able to discover in the fine print.

If you find the agent isn't franchised and you still cannot decide whether or not to sign, ask for a copy of the contract to study. Take it to one of the unions and ask the advice of their agent department or legal counseling service. They may already have heard of this agent through some of their members. If he or she has a bad record, you'll be steered away. If the contract is a poor one for you, you will be warned. Unions are on your side, and even if it appears that they are "out to get" the agent, listen to their advice. There are too many reputable agents with franchises to risk signing away your rights to a hustler.

When you decide to sign with a legitimate agency, discuss with them and fully understand ahead of time the extent and duration of your contract. Are you to be submitted in all areas? Or just commercials? How many years is the contract to cover? One? Two? More? What happens if either side wants to terminate? Can you get work on your own and not have to give them a percentage?

When you sign a franchised AFTRA or SAG contract with an agent, you may automatically terminate if you haven't received employment through the agency during any consecutive ninety-one-day period (Equity's agent-contract stipulates 120 consecutive days of no work through the agency before the actor may terminate.) Usually, if you and the agency don't work well for each other, a termination can be arranged by mutual consent.

Just because an agency has a big name in the business is no guarantee that it will be good for you. Sometimes a very small new office will get you more work and attention than a big place where you are one of hundreds of clients. This, of course, cannot be predicted ahead of time. You may not have the option of picking and choosing among several agencies. But even so, don't feel pressured to sign with anyone until you are satisfied that doing so will be an improvement on free-lancing. (Current negotiations between agents and AFTRA and SAG may lead to changes in the present agent-contracts of these two unions.)

A final word of caution on personal managers. Managers are not franchised by the unions. Signing a contract with a manager who functions as an agent is very risky. They are notorious for drawing up totally one-sided contracts and for charging exorbitant commission fees. Not all managers are cheats and out to rip you off, but don't sign a contract with one unless you first have the contract examined by a theatrical lawyer or a union representative.

You may meet some managers who want to submit you on a free-lance basis. This is probably safe, but ask them first what percentage they take if you get the job. Remember, no franchised agent currently can get more than 10 percent. There are some managers around with such bad names that just being submitted by one or using his or her name at an audition may work against you. An actor friend tells the story of a manager who submitted him for a few things until he began hearing that said manager was using every trick to get people into auditions when he hadn't been asked by the producers to submit. He was jumping the gun on agents and submitting their clients without even consulting the actors first.

Don't let yourself get squeezed into the middle of any unscrupulous manager's designs. When you sense a negative response at an audition, steer clear of the manager in the future. Try to avoid getting into his or her files in the first place.

CHAPTER 5

Auditions: What Happens and How to Prepare for Them

Auditioning can be the most exhilarating and gratifying part of an actor's life, as well as the biggest stumbling block. You may deal beautifully with interviews and agents and have a knack for getting appointments, but unless you can come through at auditions your career will stalemate.

One big factor working against you is time. You don't have a long rehearsal period to explore and play around with a role. You have to become adept at making choices quickly and following through with them. Whatever personal technique or work pattern you have evolved as an actor has to be concentrated into an audition formula. You have to learn how to get on target and stay there, sometimes with only a few minutes of preparation.

Whatever audition formula you devise must be accompanied by single-minded concentration, focusing immediately on the work at hand rather than letting nerves or surroundings or people intimidate you into stupefaction. This concentration has to stay with you from the moment you get the script until you walk into the room and convert your preparation choices into performance.

Auditions fall into two broad categories: general prepared readings, in which you choose the material and work on it ahead of time, and specific script or copy auditions, in which you are given the material a few days or only a few minutes before your audition.

General readings are used when the producer or director or agent or casting person wants to see whether your ability and quality are of interest before you are considered for anything specific. Many year-round operations such as the Chelsea Theatre (Brooklyn Academy of Music, Brooklyn) and the Phoenix Repertory Company (Lyceum Theatre, 149 West 45th Street) hold general auditions for actors and either call you back shortly after to audition for a specific production or put you on file for possible consideration later in the season.

General auditions at these theatres and others similar to them are gotten in various ways. The Stratford Shakespeare Festival (Stratford, Connecticut) has made it a practice to advertise in the trades in midwinter, asking actors interested in their summer season to submit pictures and résumés. From these submissions they choose a limited number of actors and arrange general auditions for them. Usually they request that you prepare one or two monologues of your own choosing. If they like your work at this initial appointment, you are called back and asked to prepare a specific scene from one of the plays they have scheduled for the coming season. You may have several call-backs before a decision is made.

General auditions can sometimes be arranged by your own initiative. Call the casting offices of theatres such as the American Place, the Roundabout, the Phoenix, or the Chelsea, all of whom produce three or more plays each season, and ask if, how, and when you can arrange for a general audition. You may have to follow up with several calls or visits before they begin to pay attention to you. Always try to arrange for a general audition or at least an

interview with one of the people in the casting offices of
these permanent theatres, rather than just mailing in a picture
and résumé and not following up on it.

In some cases general auditions can be arranged by an
agent. The New York Public Theatre (New York Shakespeare
Festival) schedules actors for general auditions both directly
and through agents. Since this institution is responsible for a
number of productions yearly, both in the downtown theatre
on Lafayette Street and at the Lincoln Center Theatre complex, you should find a way of making the acquaintance of
one or more of their casting personnel and getting a general
audition.

Getting into casting offices is not as difficult as you might
think—if you make more than a token effort. You might try
dropping by a theatre at an off time, during the summer or in
between casting sessions when the offices are not overloaded
with work. In some cases a phone call or a series of phone
calls will get you an appointment. Sometimes sending a flyer
for a showcase you're doing and following up with a phone
call may get someone from the office to see your show. It's
the same kind of "keeping after them" routine that was
described in the section on making the rounds. The important thing is to realize that these theatres see new actors all
the time and there's no reason that they shouldn't see you, if
you make the effort and are not put off by one or two false
starts.

Agents and casting directors of soap operas sometimes ask
actors to prepare a monologue or scene for them in addition
to coming in for a personal interview. Doing a scene means
getting another actor, choosing a good piece of material,
scheduling rehearsals, and so on. If the audition is only a
showcase for you, be sure and choose a scene that highlights
your character. If the audition is meant to be for the two of
you, choose material that has a balanced distribution of lines.

In selecting a scene for any general audition—whether for
an agent, casting director, or theatre—keep in mind that
certain pieces are done over and over again. Try to avoid
overworked selections such as the popular Neil Simon plays,
the popular Tennessee Williams and Arthur Miller works.
Choose pieces that are appropriate to the occasion. A soap

opera casting person isn't too interested in hearing Shakespeare or any of the classics. Soap opera audition pieces should not have an excess of props and should be more conversation than confrontation. Theatres of the avant-garde, experimental variety would not be excited by a commercial piece. If no preference is made clear to you, ask what kind of material would be suitable.

Try to get a director or actor friend to work with you and help shape the scene or monologue. It's difficult to criticize yourself and hard for two actors working on a scene to know if they are going in the right direction. Of course you should memorize the material. Working off book is too much of a distraction for you and the listener. If you keep within the time limit given—two to five minutes for a monologue, five to ten minutes for a scene—memorization should not be a problem.

When you do get a general audition with an agent, casting director, or a theatre, you will not always be able to tell if they liked your work and are interested in auditioning or submitting you in the future. Agents may indicate that you should "keep in touch." In that case, call them periodically and if you feel comfortable doing so, ask them to submit you for a specific production. You'll have to judge for yourself whether to press them or wait until they contact you.

As for theatres that give you a general audition, be sure and note the name of the casting person who saw you. When the theatre is casting a show containing a part you could do, call *that* person and ask him or her if you can come in for a reading.

Casting directors for soaps who have auditioned you may be called periodically unless they indicate that they don't want you to phone them. Simply ask if they have any work for you, meaning extra work. As for principal auditions, which don't come along that frequently, you may have to count on their calling you. If you should hear of an actor's leaving a show or a new part that is being cast, you can try calling and asking for an audition. Nothing ventured, nothing gained, and the worse that can happen is a "no."

General auditions are held for hundreds of actors. Even if you give a very good one, you may be forgotten unless afterward you assert yourself and gradually become a presence with a familiar name and face. Use any excuse you can think of—dropping off new pictures, "in-the-neighborhood-thought-I'd-stop-by"—to get recognition. You will have to be very persistent without becoming overbearing. It's a delicate business and you may not get any feedback for months. When in doubt, keep after them. How long? Until you get what you're after. If you sense that you have no chance of getting an audition or submission out of them after months of trying, ask the person you have closest contact with in the office if they do or don't have any interest in you. It's better to avoid this ultimatum but if all else seems to be failing, this is one way of finalizing the issue. Of course you shouldn't be indignant or testy, but make it clear that your time is valuable and you feel that you deserve an honest response. Then be prepared for and accept whatever they tell you.

Repertory companies such as the Washington Arena, Hartford Stage Company, McCarter, or the Guthrie often use the Theatre Communications Group, TCG, as their representative in New York. TCG holds general auditions on a regular basis to provide a file of actors to call when out-of-town theatres ask them to line up auditions for their season or for a specific production. To get an audition with TCG you must call or drop by their office at 15 East 41st Street and ask for one. The waiting list is usually very long and you may have to submit a picture and résumé first. Keep trying until you get an audition with TCG because they are a valuable connection to the professional theatre world outside New York. You can stop by their office any time and simply look at their bulletin board. Often notices for out-of-town productions are posted and you can write or call the theatre directly, asking for an audition.

Often this procedure is the best way of getting auditions with dinner theatres, regional theatres, repertory companies, and summer stock houses around the country. Send a letter with a picture and résumé to the theatre requesting an audition. If you are trying to get summer stock work or seasonal employment with a company, be sure to contact them early enough. In the case of summer theatre, write in January or February. Regional companies usually arrange for their fall season the preceding spring, around April or May.

You can find the names and addresses of many dinner theatres and stock and regional houses by keeping a close watch on the trades. Both *Backstage* and *Show Business* publish at regular intervals lists of Equity houses around the country. You can get lists of dinner theatres, children's theatres, summer, winter, or year-round stock theatres, and resident theatres from the Equity office.

Often out-of-town professional theatres come to New York once or twice a year to cast upcoming productions. Usually they hold an open Equity call and a few days of auditions. New York actors who have already made contact with these theatres by mail may have auditions arranged in advance. Frequently you can avoid the tedium of an open call if you make the effort to get in touch with these theatres before they get to New York and are deluged by hundreds of actors. They may respond by letter or simply call you when they first arrive and ask you to come in and read for them.

In some instances you may be asked to prepare a monologue, but most out-of-town theatres ask you to read from the scripts they have chosen for their upcoming season. If you know a few weeks ahead of time about your audition, find out what plays are being done so that you can familiarize yourself with the roles suited to your type.

Occasionally theatres unable to come to New York to audition may ask actors who get in touch with them to send tapes of monologues. An actress friend wrote a Shakespeare company in the far West, inquiring about their summer season, and was asked to submit a taped Shakespearean monologue. On the merits of that tape she was offered a place for the coming season.

Specific copy or script auditions can be broken down into two types—prepared and cold readings. In this instance "prepared" means that you are given a script or the material a few days or weeks ahead of the audition day. Obvious advantages are that you can read the entire script, make unhurried decisions on character and motivation, and go over the audition scene until you are satisfied with your work. The luxury of prepared script auditions is not necessarily to your advantage if you feel too pressured to produce a performance-level reading under these circumstances. The expectations of the listener are higher than they would be at a cold reading, but you shouldn't feel obligated to give a definitive presentation. The director intends to put in his two cents' worth during rehearsals, and he or she wouldn't want you so settled in a role that you couldn't easily alter your interpretation. Often the director will ask you to do a prepared scene a second time from a different point of view. He or she may be more interested in how you can take direction and move freely in and out of the different facets of a role than in your initial interpretation. While it is important to make definite choices about a character for a prepared audition and to go in knowing exactly what you are going to do with the scene, be ready and able to change your approach quickly if so directed. Memorize if asked or if you feel more comfort and freedom in doing so. If not, be familiar enough with the lines to avoid the distraction of losing your place.

If you are called to audition and nothing is mentioned about picking up a script, ask if you can get one before audition day. Television and film scripts are usually available for advance study. Legitimate stage productions often, but not always, give out copies ahead of time. Auditions for musicals usually require that you bring your own songs for the first audition. You may be given a number from the show to work on in advance if you get called back. Chorus (dance) auditions for musicals are on-the-spot cold auditions in which the choreographer goes through a combination for a small group of auditioners and watches them repeat it. Commercial copy is almost never available before audition day.

Cold readings mean no advance look at the script or copy except for the few minutes you get right before the audition. Those few minutes—even though they might seem incidental— are what make the difference between actors who are successful at cold readings and the majority who fail. You have to fill that short period with the same technique and concentration that you apply to any prepared audition. You have the right at any cold reading to take those few minutes with the material. If you ever are about to be rushed into an audition without being able to look over the script, politely ask that they give you a little time. If you must, excuse yourself, take the copy with you and give yourself the time you need in the rest room.

First read through the scene or copy two or three times to find out what is being said and the tone and direction of the material. In whatever time you have left, focus in on the raw outline of the character you are reading. You may want to step out into the hall and experiment with your choices by going over the scene aloud. The most important factor is making and utilizing some basic decisions about the scene and character. Even if they are wrong, you at least have something to hook into. If you have your choices to think about you are less likely to break concentration by worrying about how you're doing. Getting outside the material and listening to yourself happens when you don't have anything better to do. So give yourself a strong enough focus to keep you from losing connection with the material.

Can you overdo auditions? There is always the problem of compensating for the lack of organic feel for a role by overembellishment of externals, otherwise known as "indicating," "hamming it up," "doing schtick," and so forth. It's difficult to know if you are being too heavy with an audition or too light, especially since every director or casting person has a different set of expectations. If a general rule were possible, it might be that you should give as much reality and life to a role as your actor's instincts dictate. A director can always ask you to tone down or pull back in a second reading. But if an actor comes in with a reading that is several degrees below the desired energy level, he or she may risk making no impression at all. This rule—if it were possible, that is, to make one—can apply to all media: legitimate theatre, television, film, and commercials. However, there is a distinction that must be made. In films, television, and commercials, the camera's eye does not allow for excess. You have to bring the same life and reality to a TV or film or commercial audition that you bring to a legitimate play reading; and here the audience is not two hundred feet beyond the lights but only as far away as the camera lens. It's a question of how much to project the acting, rather than how much to act. Television, film, and commercial performers learn how to contain their technique and to match their energy level to the sensitivity of a microphone and a camera. Those two instruments pick up your output without your having to throw it out to them. Theatre auditions, on the other hand, can and should allow for the larger reach you have to make on a stage to get your acting across the footlights.

It's not so difficult to figure out what one should do in order to give a good audition. It's fine to know that if you go in with two objectives—working through the material with your personal *audition formula* and not breaking your *concentration* until you leave the building, you have done your part. But knowing is not the same as doing, especially when so much seems to be at stake and so many variables can sneak in to obstruct your plan. What if you walk in expecting to do the scene you had prepared and the director says: "I'm tired of hearing this one, let's try another"? Or suppose you should walk into a commercial audition and the response is: "You're not the right look, but go ahead and read anyway." I can recall a gruesome incident—a commercial audition for a household product—in which the copy contained directions for a pair of hands to "talk" to you as you tried to decide how you were going to deal with the party leftovers. I had the lines more or less under control, but when I got in front of the camera and two white-gloved hands were thrust into my face, I was so distracted that in two on-camera run-throughs I not only flubbed most of the lines but could not remember the name of the product.

Another nightmare incident that frequently happens to actors is being prepared to go in and give a terrific reading when the actor ahead of you (up for the same part) comes out of the room beaming: "They loved me! I got a call-back for next week." How can you keep your confidence from sagging? These kinds of things happen all the time. You are less likely to let them get the better of you if, besides your audition formula and your concentration, you bring along a lot of self-confidence and a huge dose of "let's-not-take-this-too-seriously" or "let's-enjoy-ourselves."

The realization that your world will not end if this audition is a bomb and that there are other things in life besides this particular part may at least keep you from breaking under pressure. Stay loose with the externals and throw all your energy, concentration, and seriousness into studying the script and transferring your preparation into delivery. The following illustration is a mock-up from a trade paper showing how most audition announcements look. The blurbs that production companies or casting offices send to the trades are about the same as the notification they send to agents or free-lance casting directors. From these announcements you can get a good idea of the details of different kinds of auditions. Some announcements may be only for Equity open interviews, but they almost always have a cast breakdown, listing specific audition qualifications.

UITY INTERVIEWS FOR "REX"

& 7 from 10-1 & 2-6 at Minskoff Theatre-45th B'way.

ity principal interviews for a new musical pro- by Richard Adler with music by Richard Rod- lyrics by Sheldon Harnick, book by Sherman to be directed by Edwin Sherin, will be held at nskoff Theatre, Broadway & 45 St. Casting to ie by Judy Abbott.

rs. & Fri. Mar. 6 & 7 - Equity actors 10-1 &

x" is set in the court of Henry VIII, in 16th ry England. All characters must sing. Roles: VIII - cast; Anne Boleyn- 23, young, fiery, vib- Actress playing Anne may also play Elizabeth; ine of Aragon - 40ish, plain, strong - young ter lady; Jane Seymour - 27, small, meek and ; Mary - Henry's daughter by Catherine of n. First act, she is 17. Second act she is 27; d - Henry's son by Jane Seymour, 10 years old; - court wizard, 50-60; Will Somers - Henry's and entertainer - 30-40. Agile, with comic skills; Smeaton - Court Musician - tenor or high ie - must play guitar or lute; Wolsey - small part, ter actor; Francis, King of France - Tall, good- g, preferably blonde. French accent.

tos and resumes may be submitted to Judy Ab-/o Jay Bernstein Public Relations, 157 W. 57th sting will begin immediately.

EQUITY INTERVIEWS FOR "MOVE OVER MRS. MARKHAM"

7/24 & 7/25 from 10 AM-5 PM at Showcase Studios, 950 8th Ave.

Equity principal interviews for Move Over Mrs. Markham for a bus and truck tour for 12 weeks, start- ing approximately Sept. 18th, will be held at Showcase Studios, 950 8th Ave. Producers are Gordon Crowe and Tom Mallow.

Wed. Jul. 24 & Thurs. Jul. 25-Equity actors from 10 AM-5 PM.

Roles: Alistair Spenlow - In his 20's; good looking London's latest fashionable interior decorator. Un- derneath his slightly arty exterior lurks a virile male; Sylvie Hauser - The Swiss au pair girl, a gorgeous big blonde who speaks with hardly any accent; Linda Lodge - a woman in her 30's, very vivacious but slightly scatterbrained; Philip Markham - a pleasant looking man, studious, but with a worried air which comes from years of being on the losing side of life; Henry Lodge - Successful, rakish and full of masculine confidence; Walter Pangbourne - a stiff, slightly vacu- ous (empty, blank, dull, stupid) business man between 45 and 50; Miss Smythe - an imposing "country" lady with a somewhat butterfly mind. Writer of doggy- woggy books for children; Miss Wilkinson - a 27 year old ex-deb, very pretty, kooky, with large horn- rimmed glasses.

rtisements reprinted by permission of Show Business and Backstage.

EQUITY INTERVIEW FOR "POLLY"

3/13 & 14 from 10-5 at Chelsea Theatre Center, 30 Lafayette St.

Equity principal interviews for "Polly," an 18th century sequel to "Beggar's Opera," written by John Gay with songs & tunes of the period, will be held at the Chelsea Theatre Center, 30 Lafayette St., Bklyn.
Thurs. & Fri. Mar. 13 & 14-Equity actors 10-5.
All actors must have classical training, and musical training (legit). Be prepared to sing at audition. Classical speech (diction), voice production and a background in period movement, fencing, etc. are musts.

Only following character do NOT double: Vanderbluff, Mrs. Ducat, Mrs. Trapes/actor, Polly, Indian, Morano/Macheath, Cawwawkee, Pohetohee.
Roles: Mr. Ducat - Wealthy West Indian planter - 50's. Doubles as La Guerre (a Pirate); Diana Trapes - Late 40's through 50's. Madame of a whorehouse in the West Indies, Same character as in The Beggar's Opera; Flimzy - Saucy, impertinent servant to Mrs. Trapes. (female); Mrs. Ducat - (Margaret Dumont type) - Late 40's through 50's. A strong minded, sharp tongued bitch. A shrew; Polly - Fresh eyed, spunky, charming lass. 20's; Macheath/Morano - Late 30's through 40's. Craggy, tough, mean, charmer. (Same as in Beggar's Opera); Jenny Diver - thirtyish, brazen, ambitious, tough. Doubles as Damaris, servant to Mrs. Ducat; Cawwakee - 20's. Stunningly handsome in face and form (good physique). The equivalent of a Greek God as an Indian; Pohetohee - 50's or 60's. A wise, gentle, kind noble Caesar. Handsome distinguished. An older version of his son; Vanderbluft - 50's. Crusty, tough old sea salt. Blustery pirate with opinions of his own. Doubles as The Poet; Culverin, Hacker, Capstern, Cutlace - 20's through 50's. Scurvy pirates, all deported highwaymen. Cutthroats and killers; Maid/Indian Woman. - 20's; Old Woman/ Old Indian Woman; Indian - Male. 20's, 30's; Sailor/Indian - 20's, 30's.
Note: Understudies for all major roles will be cast from within the total company. Some semi-nudity may be required of some of the roles.

"HAMLET" EQUITY INTERVIEWS

3/21 & 3/24 from 10-5 at NY Shakespeare Public Theatre, 425 Lafayette St.

The NY Shakespeare Festival will present "Hamlet!" in the Delacorte Theatre, Central Park this summer. It will be directed by Michael Rudman. Rehearsals May 21, the first public performance June 18. Equity principal interviews will be held at the Public Theatre, 425 Lafayette St.
Fri. Mar. 21 & Mon. Mar. 24- Equity interviews 10-5.
The role of Hamlet has been cast. All other roles are open. There will be a large amount of doubling. Actors & actresses will be seen for all roles.

"BLACK & WHITE & RED ALL O'

3/10 thru 3/13 from 10-1 & 2-6 at Gatchell & N Ltd., 303 West 42 St. Room 414.

This new play by Bob Barry will be produ Broadway by Gatchell & Neufeld, & directed May and Equity interviews will be held at offices, 303 West 42 St., Rm 414.
Mon. Mar. 10 thru Thurs. Mar. 13-Equity a
Cast Breakdown: Angela Forrester - Thirty-forty-five years old, elegant, witty, beautiful a have true star presence; Palmer Forrester - Late to fifty, vert trim, boyish, vain and supremely cal, a Broadway star, wicked, childish and c bastard; Ted Cotton - Angela's lover, Palmer' slick, polished, sensually handsome, some ten more younger than Angela. Appear briefly nud scene & be well built; Larry - Late 20's to ea ties. He must convince the audience that he is three people: A raving Puerto Rican junkie (in ble accent needed), a boyish, out of work acto cold blooded Mafia hit man; Gertrude Saide Forties to early fifties. Wife of a Broadway Pr Sardonic, warm, friendly. A bit of a yenta; N Saidenberg - Fifties. Broadway producer. Res the ups and downs of the business. Knowle Even warm hearted.

"RODGERS & HART, A CELEBRAT

3/10 & 11 from 10-5 at Morosco Theatre, 217 W Stage Door.

This musical will hold Equity principal interv the Morosco Theatre, Stage Door, 217 W Burt Shevelove will direct this show to be prod Broadway by Lester Osterman, Richard Horne Fearnley and Richard Lewine. Rehearsals March, to open in New York, the first part of
Mon. & Tues. Mar. 10 & 11 - Equity actor
Being sought are 12 very talented people mid-20's who can sing and move extremely we must be very strong dancers. Must have per and charm and exuberance. Must be versatile aginative. People must have a well-scrubbed

SAG PERFORMERS SOUGH

Zabriskie Productions, 1313 Madison Ave., accepting photos from tall, lean and lanky SA actors to play a Backwoodsman type for a sho film to be shot this spring. Must feel comforta the outdoors, and be able to relate to 4 ten kids. Age range: mid-thirties to mid-forties. Pl not phone or visit, or send photos if you do n this description. If your phone is out, due to th the phone company, and you do not have a please *do* include your address or an alternate n
Zabriskie Productions would also like tap SAG women who have distinctive voices a la thur, Tammy Grimes, etc. and SAG male vo can project Gloom and Doom.

CHORUS CALLS

"JESUS CHRIST SUPERSTAR"

5 at 3 PM at Showcase Studios, 950 8th Ave.
nis is a replacement call for Equity male & female singers which will
eld at Showcase Studios, 950 8th Ave.
nurs. Mar. 6- Equity male & female singers 3 PM.
ccomparist provided, bring your own music.

"OKLAHOMA"

10 at 10 & 2, 3/11 at 10 & 2 at Showcase Studios, 950 8th Ave.
norus audition (Equity) for "Oklahoma" to be directed by John
nley, conducted by Jay Blackton, choreographer, Robert Pagent for
s Beach, will be held at Showcase Studios, 950 8th Ave.
on. Mar. 10- Equity male singers 10 AM.
on. Mar. 10 - Equity female singers 2 PM.
ues. Mar. 11- Equity male dancers 10 AM.
ues. Mar. 11- Equity female dancers 2 PM.

MILLIKEN SHOW CASTING

*3/10 at   9 . 3/11 at 2, 3/10 at 2, 3/11 at 4:30, 3/12 at 9:30 AM at
Mark Hellinger Theatre, Broadway and 51st St.*

ne 1975 Milliken Breakfast Show will go into rehearsal on Apr. 28,
the first performance on May 28 & the final performance on June 12.
Milliken Breakfast Show schedule is such that there will be no
lict with Broadway performances.
quity chorus auditions will be held at the Mark Hellinger Theatre,
St. & B'way.
on. Mar. 10-Equity female singer/dancers from   9 AM .   All
it must be prepared to sing and dance. Piano accompaniment will be
ided. All talent will be judged by the following standards: Since this
imarily a fashion presentation of manufacturers' garments for the
the entire cast must have good appearance. It is recommended that
uditioning talent come well groomed. Dress sizes 8, 9 & 10. Must
singing, dancing, line reading, acting talents.
ues. Mar. 11 - Equity male dancers at 2 PM.
ed. Mar. 12 - Open girl children who are singer/dancers at 9:30 AM.
alent will be judged by the above standards. Childrens' dress sizes 6,
1 10.
en calls: Mon. Mar. 10-Female chorus at 2 PM.
ues. Mar. 11-Male chorus at 4:30 PM.
ed. Mar. 12-Girl children at 9:30 AM.

ACTRESS ATHLETE WANTED

Sport adventure film seeking beautiful actress to play
athletic, educated girl (20-25) who can ski and surf —
feature film will be shot on location in Africa, Mexico,
Hawaii, and across the U.S. Production starts May 1.
Send photos and resumes to Sports Adventure Films,
Ltd., 538 E. Alameda Ave., Denver, Colorado
80209. . .ADVT

LEAVES OF GRASS FOR OFF B'WAY

Equity principal interviews
have been scheduled for a Fall
production of LEAVES OF
GRASS. The musical will be
co-directed by Stanley Harte
and Bert Michaels, with Mr.
Michaels serving as choreographer.
Interviews will be held at
Celebrity Arts, 29 W. 57th,
Thursday June 3 and Thursday
June 10 from noon until 6 pm.
ROLES AVAILABLE:
White male: Mid 20s, must sing
legit extremely well and be
able to move.
White male: 30ish, must sing
and move well, and be able to
handle Whitman's poetry.
Black male: Must sing legit
and move well, mid 20s.
Black female: Mid-20s, legit
soprano and do gospel work.
White female: Mid 20s or
younger, legit soprano with
heavy stress on head voice,
must move well.
Producers are New Era Prod.,
1501 B'way, 868 27 05.

Agency Casting O. Preminger's New Film

General extras for Otto Pre-
minger's "SUCH GOOD
FRIENDS" are now being
sought by Talent Services
Associates, Inc.
Also needed are stand-ins for
Dyan Canon and James Coco.
Send photos and resumes to
TSA, 1200 B'way, 10001.
July filming.   Interviews
forthcoming. SAG only.

Advertisements reprinted by permission of *Show Business* and *Backstage*.

"FALLEN ANGELS" OPEN INTERVIEW

Equity interviews for an off-Broadway production of Noel Coward's "Fallen Angels" will be held Thursday, June 3, from 11 to 6.

This will be at the Sheridan Square Playhouse, 7th and West 4th.

ROLES:

JANE: 30's, attractive, nice personality.

SAUNDERS: 35-40, maid, should play piano and sing.

WILLY: 35, stodgy, attractive.

FRED: 35, excitable.

MAURICE: 35, French, handsome man about town.

CENTER STAGE AUDITIONS

Center Stage, Equity Lort Baltimore's resident professional theater company, will hold auditions in Baltimore for its 1975-76 season on April 21, 22, and 23. Actors interested in auditioning should mail their résumé and picture to Center Stage *no later than April 1*. After the resumes and request for an audition have been received, the candidate will be notified of the time and place of the auditions *by mail* the week of April 7. Also at this time, the actor will be informed of the desired length and content of the audition. Actor resumes will not be accepted after April 1 for the April audition time. Resumes and pictures should be submitted to Vandy Rioux, Center Stage, 31 E. North Avenue, Baltimore, Maryland 21202.

Center Stage will be attending the spring Theatre Communication Group National Student Auditions in New York City, Washington, D.C., Boston and Chicago.

ACTRESS FOR TV COMMERCIAL

Accepting Actress - singer - dancer combination photos (full length) for a National TV Commercial to be filmed in Florida. Girl chosen must be free to travel for a year to represent sponsor in showcases. Qualifications: Approximately 5'5", 110 lbs-fresh, wholesome American girl look. Send resume immediately to International Advertising Services, Pioneer Playhouse, Danville, Kentucky 40422. . . .ADVT.

WANTS JACKIE GLEASON LOOK-ALIKE FOR FILM

Ballyhooist Dick Falk, will be pitchin' "The Life and Times of Maxie Stevens," a farce authored by George Q. Lewis, about a Newark, New Jersey pitchman who ran a harem for himself and buddies, based on the early life of a current top comic. Yuri Zabran, real estate magnate and airport developer, will underwrite the venture for an October premiere at a "middle" theatre set up.

They are seeking an early look alike for Gleason. If you look like Gleason did in 1940 send your picture to Dick Falk 220 W. 42nd.

TOM WARD CASTING COLLEGE CAMPUS FILM

The Tom Ward Agency is now casting a new film, CAMPUS, produced by Star-Trek Productions, to be filmed at a university on Long Island.

CAMPUS is based on incidents that took place at Kent State.

Some minimal nudity may be involved but no sex acts will be shown.

Phil Morini, at Tom Ward, will cast all principals, bits, and extras. Needed are girls,17-23, wholesome, good looking, midwest college kids, no high fashion types.

Males should be tall, good looking football player types, both bearded and clean shaven.

Phil Morini will see actors from 2 to 5 pm at the Tom Ward Agency, 460 West 54 St. Bring photos, resumes and SAG card. Actors may also be submitted by agents.

Shooting for CAMPUS is set to start in mid-August.

Advertisements reprinted by permission of *Show Business* and *Backstage*.

STRAIGHT "LEGIT" AUDITIONS

The auditions for straight productions—whether Broadway, Off-Broadway, dinner theatre, regional, repertory, or children's theatre—are held in theatres, the producer's offices, or rented rehearsal studios. Places such as the Public Theatre, which has two facilities, the Lafayette Street complex and Lincoln Center, and the Chelsea in Brooklyn, the Circle in the Square on 50th Street and Broadway, and the American Place at 46th Street and Avenue of the Americas all have, besides one or more stages, large rehearsal rooms where most of the auditioning takes place.

Generally, out-of-town productions rent a rehearsal studio or the offices of a New York producer for their auditions. Some companies rent out space in hotels or public facilities such as a YMCA. If the theatre is casting through TCG—the Theatre Communications Group—they use the TCG space on East 41st Street. Low-budget Off-Off Broadway, including showcase productions, if their theatre isn't free, may hold auditions in apartments or, if it is a university-connected show, at the school's facilities. The Equity Library Theatre (ELT), a respected showcase housed in a large buildling on Riverside Drive and 103rd Street, holds auditions for their productions—six or more yearly—at their theatre. Getting an audition with ELT, if you are an Equity member, simply involves going to the Equity office and signing up for an appointment.

The legitimate straight audition usually consists of doing a scene or scenes from the script. As noted earlier, you may be able to see the script and work over the audition pieces in advance or you may have a cold reading. In some initial auditions you may be asked to do an improvisation or something other than a direct reading from the script. When auditions for *Story Theatre* were held, actors were asked to come in with their adaptation of a fable or parable.

When you go into the audition you can expect to find the director or his or her assistant, or perhaps the producer and/or playwright. Sometimes actors already cast sit in, as well as stage managers and casting personnel. If you have been asked to prepare a scene, you will probably read with the stage manager or an actor if there is one available. Usually readers try to be as unobtrusive and accommodating as possible to the auditioners. But occasionally their extremely bland and monotone line-feeding is a drawback. You have to expect less than ideal help from them.

Mastering the technical aspects of auditioning takes time and experience. Classes are given on how to audition and it might be worth your while to take one, if you don't feel secure about auditioning or if your acting class or school did not prepare you for them adequately. However, there are a few basic strategies that can see you through until you are more relaxed about auditions. The first "must" is to take your time. Leave unnecessary bags and coats, umbrellas and parcels, and so on outside the audition room, if it's safe. If you have to take everything in with you, put them down close to the door out of the way so that you can pick them up as you leave. Be sure to take in your picture and résumé if they are needed.

There may be a little conversation before your audition to put you at ease or to provide background information on the play. When the time comes to audition, check out the space before you begin. Make sure you have enough room and move any furniture into position or out of the area altogether. If you are asked to read from a chair, be sure it is placed far enough away from the listeners. Unless you are specifically requested to stay put, feel free to move out of the seat if so motivated. Often it's easier in a first reading to stay in one position, but movement, if you feel like it, is fine. In fact, you may be asked to move around as much as the script or your actor's instincts dictate.

Before you speak take a moment or two to calm yourself and focus in on the character and situation. Once you begin, try not to listen to yourself and if you skip a line or trip over a word, don't be concerned. *Don't stop* and break concentration by asking to start again. This is amateurish and unnecessary unless you have really gotten off to a bad start. When you finish, end the reading in character. Don't do any editorializing, by facial expression or gesture, on what you've just done. Why demean yourself or the material? Leave the criticism to the listener. Either before or after a reading, avoid making excuses for yourself, such as: "I have a terrible cold," "I'm not very good at comedy," "I didn't understand what the character meant." If you have any questions about the material, ask for clarification *before* you give your reading. If you are asked to do a scene a second time from a different point of view or with an altered motivation, take the time to understand and digest the suggestion before you start up again. As has been mentioned, directors are often more interested in how you can take their suggestions and work with them and in how flexible you are than in your initial interpretation.

When the audition is over, the best procedure is a quick, polite, confident exit. If they want to tell you something about call-backs, they will. If they want to write down some more information, they will ask. If you must know how soon the decision will be made because of other pending jobs, ask for an estimate of how long it will be before call-backs or final casting. Explain that you have other commitments and need to know, within a certain number of days, if they are interested. Don't go through this routine if it's not the truth, just to get information out of them. No one likes to be pressured, especially under these circumstances. Don't press for a decision unless you do have a potential conflict.

SINGING AUDITIONS

Musical auditions are held at a theatre or studio with a piano available. If a large theatre is used, the applicants usually gather and wait their turn in the backstage area. The auditions take place on stage with the casting personnel in the house. If the theatre is small, those auditioning may wait in the outside lounge of the theatre. Usually singing auditions at theatres are held on stage unless there is a piano available in a rehearsal room of the theatre. Rehearsal studios frequently are rented by musical productions for their singing and dance auditions. About five or six studios in town are used over and over again and, unfortunately, they are in general poorly adapted for accommodating large crowds. Often singers crowd into a tiny hallway or stairwell or outer room within earshot of the auditions.

As you can see, the cast breakdowns for musicals include

the specific range the musical demands for each role, in some cases even noting the high and low notes the singer must have. This information must have a strong influence on your choice of material for an initial audition. If a role calls for a belt style, you should come in with a belt number. Fit the song you choose to the character description as well as the singing range. For instance, if the character is described as "tall, slender, beautiful, cool, elegant, sophisticated legit soprano," the choice of song should fit the type. You wouldn't choose the same number if the character is described as "jolly but sharp-tongued, stout, energetic character soprano." In some cases singers are asked to bring two contrasting numbers, an up tune, perhaps, and a ballad. Your selections of music are very important and have almost as much influence on your audition outcome as your voice.

Singing coaches are very helpful as you build up a repertoire for auditions. If you can't study with one regularly, try and get in a session before any important singing audition. Not only do singing coaches improve your audition technique and style, but they frequently know exactly the right number to choose for particular auditions. If you can't go to a singing coach, at least try to locate a good pianist to go over your number with you. Some singers like to bring their own accompanist to auditions. Most singing auditions provide an accompanist, but you can never be sure of his or her skill, adaptability, or familiarity with your song. Many a singer has botched an audition because of a mix-up with the accompanist. That's why singers like to bring along their own pianists, as much for moral as for musical support.

There is little mystery about singing auditions. You simply get up and do the song or songs you have prepared. On occasion you may be asked to run through some scales with the pianist or to try doing some music from the show. (Don't use a number from the show for your initial audition, but you should have one from the show prepared to do if requested.) Frequently you will be stopped before you finish your number—either because the listener is rushed or running late, likes you and doesn't need to hear more, or knows that you are not right for the show. The only way to know which of these applies is by what they tell you or don't tell you.

You may be asked to come back for another audition immediately after you finish your number, you may be called that evening or the following day or in a week or more, or you may be told "thank you very much" and nothing more.

Dance—chorus—calls, as you can see from the mock-up ads, may be held in conjunction with singing auditions or separately from the other auditions for a show. Almost always male and female dance auditions are held at different times. If anything special is required, such as tap or jazz or singers who dance or dancers who sing, the ad will indicate it. As was mentioned earlier, dance auditions for chorus consist of the choreographer or an assistant demonstrating a combination or set of combinations and watching the dancers, separated into small groups, repeat the steps. The choreographer may then pull out the dancers he or she likes and let the others go. More combinations, more eliminations, until a handful of dancers remain. Often you know right then or soon after if you have the job.

Not all singing and dance auditions are for musicals. Often dancers and singers are used in commercials or industrials (an advertisement or commercial done as a large theatrical production), nightclub routines, or on sea cruises. These specialized auditions are not always advertised in the trades but handled through agents or strictly through connections. For instance, a choreographer who is doing the dance numbers for an industrial may simply choose a group of people he or she has worked with before or known of professionally. Likewise, voice-over singing work on commercials is usually handled through agents and infrequently advertised in the trades.

FILMS

Auditions for principal roles in SAG films (all actors are members of Screen Actors Guild) are not usually advertised through the trades, but a cast breakdown similar to the one shown in the mock-up is sent out to agents and casting directors. They submit actors who fit the descriptions and these actors go through more or less the same audition process described in the legitimate-audition section. Film producers may schedule interviews before auditions, since an actor's style and look in real life may make a big difference in his or her "rightness" for the part.

Agents usually secure film scripts for actors to study at least a day in advance of the auditions. If no copies are available prior to audition day, you will have to make the best of a cold reading. Sometimes only "sides" are given out to actors as they arrive. A side is a page or more from the script—the audition scene and nothing else. Ask to see a complete script anyway, and, if you don't have time to scan all of it, at least check out the first few pages for cast descriptions and background material. Find where your audition scene comes in and try to establish its context by looking at the surrounding scenes. If you can't get a script, do your best with the side. You're not at any more of a disadvantage than the other actors.

Film scripts contain a lot of extraneous material, such as directions for camera shots, lighting, background music, and so forth. Be sure to go through the scene carefully and note where dialogue continuity is broken by technical directions. Know where these inserts occur so that they don't catch you off guard and interfere with a smooth reading.

First auditions for films are almost never on camera. You may be auditioned at the producer's office, the film company's studio, the casting director's office, or a rented space in a hotel or rehearsal hall. Even early call-backs are seldom on camera but may be for the director, who often does not sit in on first auditions. If you survive several call-backs, chances are that you and the other actors up for the same part will be given screen tests. (This is not done for minor speaking parts or extra work.) You are given adequate time to prepare the scene; it is often the same one you read at early auditions. You'll be made up, maybe costumed, and possibly directed. After that it's simply a question of who wins out in the screening room.

Extras in films are often cast through the trades. Interviews such as the one in the mock-up ad are held by casting directors or the producers, and usually hundreds of actors show up. The ad may stipulate that only SAG members will be seen and you may or may not be asked to show your union card.

Nonunion films seldom pay principals and extras as well as union operations, and they don't have to guarantee a limited demand on your time. SAG allows a producer eight hours per day from actors and insists on overtime pay.

Principals in industrial films are usually cast through agents, though some producers advertise in the trades. The audition procedure for industrials is a simplified version of what's just been described. Actors may be cast after first readings or in first call-backs. There is seldom any on-camera auditioning for industrial films. They are not usually feature-length and shooting time can run from a few days to several weeks for longer scripts. Both AFTRA and SAG have negotiated industrial film contracts, and one or the other will be used if it's a union film.

TELEVISION

Television auditions for principals in soaps, series, or specials are never advertised in the trades. Each show or series has a casting director who either calls actors already familiar to him or her (by reputation or previous professional contact) or asks agents for submissions. (In some cases, actors who have managed to get in to see these casting directors and been used for extra work may be asked, in time, to audition for a principal role or at least may be able to request an audition.) The writers provide a cast breakdown containing physical descriptions and pertinent casting information. Agents and free-lance casting directors receive a copy and follow the usual submission procedure.

First auditions are usually in the office of the casting director, either at the TV studio or at the advertising agency that handles the show for the sponsor. Probably only the casting director and/or assistant sits in on first readings. On call-backs actors read for producer, director, and/or writer. Final contenders for a role may be put on videotape before a decision is made. If so, the actors are carefully made up and

coifed, perhaps costumed, and put before the camera with or
without directorial assistance.

Audition scenes are usually available for study a few days
in advance, perhaps longer. Some casting directors use cold
readings for first auditions and then give actors a scene to
prepare for a call-back. TV audition scenes may be edited and
free of technical directions, but if a normal script is used, be
prepared for extraneous technical material interspersed with
dialogue.

COMMERCIALS

Auditions for commercials are different in several ways
from the four types already discussed. First, a different sort
of acting skill peculiar to commercials is needed; second,
many first auditions are *on camera* with cue cards or a
teleprompter, and that can be unsettling to the inexperienced
commercial auditioner. Finally, the content of commercial
copy is never anything more than what it has to be—an
advertisement meant to sell a product, and frequently not
artistically or even intellectually stimulating to the actor who
has to read it. Anyone who decides that he or she wants to
get work in commercials has to acquire the special skill, learn
to deal with the camera, and learn to like reading the copy.

Probably the quickest way of learning how to audition
well is to go to one of the reputable "how-to" commercial
schools in the city. You can expect to pay about one to two
hundred dollars for eight to twelve classes. Ask other actors,
agents, or advertising agency casting directors for recommendations. Be sure the school you choose has video equipment and on-camera practice guaranteed for each class and a
limited number of students per class. Always ask to audit
before signing up, and try to visit more than one school
before deciding.

If you'd rather learn "on the job," that is, simply by going
to several commercial auditions and gradually assimilating the
technique, be prepared for a difficult adjustment period and
several lost auditions. Very few actors come by commercials
naturally. Don't expect that it's easy to pick up commercial

know-how or that once you have it you'll automatically begin getting jobs. Estimates range from one job out of every twenty auditions to one job out of every one hundred auditions for the average commercial actor.

Commercial calls are almost never advertised in the trades, though a few specialty ads such as the ones in the mock-up appear from time to time. Advertising agencies either rely on their own files or ask their favorite agents for submissions. Calls for commercials may go out a few days in advance of, sometimes the day before, or even the morning of the audition. Enterprising and experienced commercial actors may go to as many as four or five auditions daily.

Commercial auditions are held frequently at the office of the advertising agency handling the product or the studio of the intermediary free-lance casting director, if one is used. Auditions are scheduled every ten minutes or so and it's a good idea to come early. As actors arrive they are given the copy and called in to the audition room as their turn comes up. Depending on the number of actors and the size of the studio or office, space may or may not be a problem. If possible, try to find a solitary corner in which to work over the copy. If necessary, go out into the hall for privacy. Find out if there will be a cue card or TelePrompTer. If not, decide if you are going to memorize the copy or take it in with you. Many commercial actors learn how to memorize quickly after several auditions, but if you are insecure about memorization, take the copy in with you and work with it.

If the audition is to be videotaped, you may be given one or two dry run-throughs and the listener may suggest alterations in your reading. When the camera starts rolling you'll be asked to "slate," which means that you give your name, the take number, and go right into the copy. Everything is over quickly and you often don't get to try again. The copy may be only twenty or thirty seconds long, but you have to put everything into those few words. One successful commercial actress friend has said that when she makes an "attitude" choice about the character and the copy content and follows through with her interpretation, she usually gets positive feedback. Often the agency people don't know what the person in the copy is like and are waiting for one of the actors to show them an interesting possibility. Her theory is that it's better to make an imaginative character choice and go with it than to sit on the fence. Even if it's wrong, it will stand out from the rest of the auditions and may at least get you a call-back.

Not every commercial audition is on camera. You may not even get any copy until you pass an appearance test. Agencies frequently just want to look at actors, and auditions won't go beyond that if you don't fit their concept of how the character should look.

Call-backs for commercials can be more agonizing than most. If the copy is very short or the first audition was a week or so earlier, you may not be able to recall and re-create what you did the first time. The more call-backs you have—there can be as many as four or five for one commercial—the more confusing and nerve-wracking they can become. Should you try something new, or do what you did the first time or the second time? You can only go by what your instincts dictate at the moment and hope that your final choice pleases the sponsors and they decide to go with you.

THE BIG LETDOWN

You sometimes prepare an audition for days and it's all over in a matter of minutes. You sometimes are told: "Terrific, you'll hear from us tomorrow," and you never do. You sometimes give an awful audition and hate yourself for weeks. How do you cope? How do you forget what's past and move on to the next audition? If you can't live through the aftermath—the worst part of auditions—you'll never make it as an actor. You have to learn to understand why you didn't get the part, accept that fact, step away from the whole experience, and start fresh with something else.

Sometimes you will audition poorly. If you were a computer, you could expect perfection; but you're not and you must give yourself room for occasional failures. They happen to everyone and they do only as much damage as you allow them. The person who sees your bad auditions forgets them soon enough. You must forget them too.

What about the times when you thought you did well and you never heard anything? These auditions are more frustrating than the ones you know you flubbed. You can torture yourself for days, trying to figure out what you did or said that lost it for you. If you know that you did your best at an audition, do yourself a favor and blame someone or something else, not yourself, when you don't get the job. Think of all the variables over which you have no control. The producer insists that the sponsor's daughter do the commercial. The money doesn't come through and the production is cancelled. Another actor as good as you comes along who worked with the director before. The director wants a Mediterranean type and you're Nordic. Fat/thin, short/tall, middle-aged/twenties—if you're the wrong one and don't fit the director's or producer's concept of the character, you probably will be passed by. There are too many good actors around of every type for producers to compromise and go with someone who doesn't quite look the part. It's a buyer's market.

Forget your bad auditions. If you can figure out what got in your way—tension, lack of adequate preparation, poor concentration—try to correct it the next time. Don't worry about the person who saw you. There are thousands of actors who have all given poor readings and hundreds of casting people who see bad auditions every day. Is yours really so exceptionally awful that it will make theatre history?

As for the good auditions you give that don't lead anywhere, don't discount their long-range value. No good audition is a waste of time. While casting directors tend to forget the bad and mediocre auditions, they usually remember the good ones. And they do call back actors for other jobs weeks, months, sometimes a year or two later—because they remember. Even if they don't call you, you may run into them at another audition or interview and they'll say: "Oh, yes, I remember you. I liked your reading." It happens just that way, many times.

CHAPTER 6

Working

The more acting jobs you get the more you realize that the unions define and protect your rights more than any employer. The contracts that AFTRA, Equity, and SAG have negotiated over the years for actors, the rigid overseeing of productions, the exposure and correction of unfair employer practices, and the various fringe benefit plans have all contributed to the betterment of the actor's lot. This last chapter briefly will sort out the particulars of the three major actors' unions and explain how they can help you, and end with a look at some nonunion work opportunities.

AFTRA

AFTRA's (American Federation of Television and Radio Artists) constitution states that it will

> advance, foster, promote and benefit all those connected with performances in the fields of radio, television and

phonograph recordings . . . ; assist such persons in securing
just and equitable contracts, agreements, working conditions and minimum compensation in their dealings with employers, producers, networks, stations, advertising agencies,
sponsors, independent packagers, transcription companies,
phonograph recording companies, agents, managers, im-
presarios and others connected directly or indirectly with the
radio, television or phonograph record business.

The following chart illustrates a few of the scale wage
contracts negotiated by AFTRA. (All rates are subject to
change as the unions see fit to promote increases.)

Network Prime-time Dramatic Programs

Day actor	$172.50
3-day actor (1/2-hour or 1-hour show)	440.00
(1–1/2-hour show)	517.00
Weekly actor	604.00
Multiple Programs—Weekly	
(1/2 hour or 1 hour)	405.00
(1–1/2 hour)	477.50
Series	
1/2 hour	604.00
1 hour	725.00
1–1/2 hour	966.00

Network Non-prime-time Dramatic Programs

More than 5 Lines

15 minutes or less	128.00
15 minutes to 30 minutes	211.00
30 minutes to 60 minutes	267.50
60 minutes to 90 minutes	337.50
90 minutes to 120 minutes	407.50

Under 5 Lines

15 minutes or less	78.50
15 minutes to 30 minutes	99.00
30 minutes to 60 minutes	122.50
60 minutes to 90 minutes	139.00
90 minutes to 120 minutes	159.00

Walk-ons and Extras

15 minutes or less	32.00
15 minutes to 30 minutes	55.50

30 minutes to 60 minutes	71.00
60 minutes to 90 minutes	86.00
90 minutes to 120 minutes	102.00

Radio Rates

	Broadcast fee	Rebroadcast fee
5 minutes or less	33.50	11.50
5 minutes to 15 minutes	35.50	17.00
15 minutes to 30 minutes	52.00	21.00
30 minutes to 60 minutes	69.00	29.50

Television Commercials

Principals

Day	165.90
Cumulative total + residuals for 13-week cycle	1003.80

Extras

Hand Model	189.00
General extra	126.00

EQUITY

Equity's constitution pledges "to advance, promote, foster and benefit all those connected with the 'art of theatre' . . . particularly the profession of acting and the conditions of persons engaged therein."

The following are the current weekly rates Equity has negotiated for the various types of theatrical production.

Production Contract—Broadway Minimum

Pt. of origin	Away from pt. of origin (on tour)
$245.00	$347.50

Off-Broadway Contract

Box office gross up to	Salary
6500.00	150.00

on a sliding scale to
$13,000.00 box office gross

League of Resident Theatres—LORT Contract

A size house	202.45
B size house	176.20
C size house	158.70
D size house	137.50

Stock

Outdoor musical	168.00 (Resident)
Indoor musical	193.47
Non-resident dramatic	188.32
Resident dramatic	190.00 (X size)
	154.00 (Y size)
	140.00 (Z size)

Dinner Theatre

Small house	135.00
Medium house	165.00
Large house	190.00

Children's Theatre

Weekly	115.82
Per performance	20.08

Industrial Shows

7-Day	380.19
1st Day	131.08
each day after	97.71

Cabaret

Per week	192.50

SAG (SCREEN ACTORS GUILD)

The objects of Screen Actors Guild as stated in its constitution are:

To represent and coordinate the activities of the various persons . . . engaged or employed . . . as actors in the motion picture industry. . . . The term 'motion picture industry' includes without limitation, the production of motion pictures by any means or devices for theatrical, television, industrial, educational, commercial, advertising or religious purposes or uses.

The following are some of the current scale contracts negotiated by SAG.

Theatrical Film

Principal Actors

Day	$172.50
Weekly	604.00

Extras (day rate)

General	46.00
Special ability	56.00
Silent bit	94.00

Industrial and Educational Films

Day	172.50
Weekly	604.00

Television Motion Pictures

Day	172.50
Weekly	604.00

Commercials

Principal Actors

Day	165.90
Cumulative total + residuals for 13-week cycle	852.60
Voice-over	123.90

Extras

Hand model	189.00
General extra	126.00

PROBLEMS ON THE JOB

There has always been a potential for friction between actors and management. Every company has its share of complaints on both sides. Usually the problems can be referred to a union official either by the elected deputy (an actor chosen by all the actors as their liaison) or the affected actor or producer for arbitration and settlement. Various difficulties that arise during production include disputes over salary, rehearsal and performance schedules, individual or wholesale dismissal or firing, backstage and living accommodations, vacation time, payments into unemployment insurance, and countless others. The unions have dealt with almost every conceivable problem and worked out a reasonable rule to settle any question brought forward by actors or management. As long as you are in a union-contracted production, your rights cannot be continually ignored or abused unless you neglect to bring the breach to the attention of the proper union. And the producer expects that you will adhere to the terms set forth in the contract or face union censure.

There are those problems inherent to the acting profession over which unions, management, and actors have little or no control: poor box-office sales, closing before opening, cancellation of production by networks or sponsors, elimination of parts through script revisions, theatre collapse (literally) or, to put it another way, termination. Single job security in the usual sense of lifetime or at least yearly duration exists only in a few instances for the professional actor. You go from one job to another, often with an unbearably long gap in between. For these problems there is no solution—except to start the search all over again and try to keep the time "in between jobs" as short as possible.

UNION BENEFITS

The pension and welfare (health and life insurance) funds of the three unions and the Actors' Fund are the major benefit plans available to actors.

If you are employed for eight weeks or less under an Equity Production (Broadway) contract, you receive six months free health and life insurance coverage; if employed more than eight weeks but less than six months, you will be covered during the period of employment and for six months following the last day of your employment in the production; if employed more than six months, you are covered during employment and for nine months thereafter. Other types of Equity contracts provide coverage for shorter durations of time. If members are not employed they may pay a quarterly premium and receive the same coverage accruing to working members.

Both AFTRA and SAG offer health and welfare benefits to members who have earned $1000 or more under AFTRA or SAG contracts within a period of twelve consecutive months. This coverage continues from year to year as long as you have $1000 or more reported earnings during the appropriate base period.

Each union provides free services for members, ranging from passes for a new pair of shoes for about two hundred Equity members every six months (first come, first served) to free commercial classes for interested paid-up AFTRA members. Equity provides a survival job list to members, available at the Green Room reception desk. The unions also provide free legal counsel, unemployment insurance information, credit unions, and several other actor-oriented benefits.

The Actors' Fund is an institution founded to assist the needy in the profession. The only requirement to receive aid is that the applicant should be able to show that his or her primary source of livelihood has been from some branch of the entertainment field and that he or she currently cannot provide for basic necessities. For specific information write to the Actors' Fund of America, 1501 Broadway, New York, N.Y. 10036.

NONUNION WORK

For the gaps in between acting jobs you should explore the possibility of field-related work—usually nonunion and not quite acting, but better than most part-time employment. Print work (photography advertising for magazines, newspapers, trade publications) is one such actor fill-in. Some agencies have special print divisions that submit actors to advertising agencies or photographers, but as yet no union or standard work rules have been established to protect and provide for actors working in those fields. Usually print jobs last for one day or a few hours and actors make around a hundred dollars flat fee—usually "off the books" with a ninety-day wait for the money. Print work may give you good national or regional exposure and it's not a bad way to make a few dollars even though you don't get any kind of residual pay, as you do with commercials.

Working in live industrial shows, nontheatrical, as a host or hostess or at display booths is a frequent in-between job actors like. The pay is about fifty dollars per day and can extend from one to ten days or so. Sometimes companies advertise for actors in the trades or go through agents. Naturally it helps if you have a beautiful or handsome modellike look, since the idea is to have personable "pretty" people to display merchandise or chat with buyers.

Modeling is a helpful sideline if you have the physical qualifications—tall, slim, and attractive. Women now can be more natural, a little heavier, and real-looking, and men with a rougher, not-so-smooth look—even bearded or balding—are more acceptable than before. However, modeling is a difficult business to break into and requires almost full-time involvement. Beginning models face the same rounds-making, self-sell routine as actors. Occasionally you may be able to secure a part-time job modeling in a showroom in the garment district or a few days' employment with a photographer or illustrator. If you think you have modeling potential and are interested in developing it, pick up some of the "how-to" publications or call a few modeling agencies for suggestions.

If you have difficulty with an employer in any nonunion job such as print work, industrials, or modeling, your only recourse is to ask the agent or manager who got you the job to intercede. If you secured the job on your own, you'll have to live with the consequences—unless you can clear up the misunderstanding by direct confrontation. Usually nonunion job squabbles center around money. You may be told you're to get $100 for the day and you get a check for $50. A photographer may hire you for a print job on location, for instance, at Kennedy Airport, and you end up paying for your transportation to and fro. You can ask for reimbursement but, if refused, you can't complain to anyone. There is no union to speak up for you and see that you are not cheated. Try to get a written salary agreement ahead of time and ask for transportation or other costs before the job starts. You are on your own and if you get burned on one or two nonunion jobs, take necessary precautions the next time.

CONCLUSION

This book has attempted to give some concrete and useful information to people who want to make it as professional actors in New York. Unfortunately, books can only be read and put aside. They can't do for you anything more than give you the incentive to do for yourself. Books about acting cannot plot out each individual's road to "stardom" or even begin to make the realities of the profession less of an ordeal. There is nothing easy about making it as an actor and there are very few successful actors around who haven't paid dearly in one way or another for their success.

That old cliché about "no overnight success stories" is the truest cliché of them all. It takes years, literally years, to launch an acting career. The first few are probably the most difficult, not necessarily because you work any harder, but because the returns on your work are usually very slim. Fortunately, the newness and excitement of beginning dull the grim and disheartening aspects of the acting life. Going through the first years of struggle is probably never as awful at the time as it is in retrospect. The showcases, the prospect of meeting agents, the appointments, the first Equity interviews and auditions—all these things, when they are new to you, are almost enough gratification in themselves. When something really good does happen—your first job—the effort you put into the means to the end seems worth the huge investment of your time and energy. The pleasure of getting a job, of knowing that you auditioned better than hundreds of others, negates the importance and nearly obliterates the memory of the countless failures that came before.

More than anything else it's the delight of getting a job, even though, especially in the early years, the times are few, that keeps you going and feeds your fantasy. The idea of anyone's coming to New York, beating the odds and making it as an actor is, after all, a fantastic contemplation. As long as you can keep alive and urgent that desire to realize your fantasy, you can last. And the longer you last, the greater your endurance, the more likely you are to succeed. The cornerstone of most acting careers is tenacity.

If you can survive the first year or two on very little encouragement—on one job, or two, or a handful of jobs, and get enough creative stimulus from acting, singing, and dance classes and showcase work, and if you go after jobs with a consistent drive, you are bound to get more work than you did in the beginning. It's misleading to say that you are bound to start getting steady employment. No actor can ever be sure of his next job until he signs the contract. No one can predict if the years to come will be especially good for actors—as were the fifties, when television was in its infancy and people worked "all the time"—or like the late sixties and early seventies, which have been written off as "depressed."

An optimistic forecast would be that after the first few years of active involvement in the profession you can expect steady sporadic employment. If you can build on this tentative foundation with your own determination and muster outside help, such as agents, and if you have a bit of luck, you may reach the bottom of the top. To put it another, less equivocal, way, you may reach the "making it" plateau, meaning that you are surviving financially from acting work, that you do a little less pursuing and are occasionally sought after for jobs and that you are known and respected by your colleagues and employers within the profession. This is the level that most successful actors reach—recognition inside the profession, but not public-figure status or, if you will, stardom.

Stardom—national recognition, being a name performer—occurs infrequently and yet often enough to tantalize most actors in the business. Not everyone wants that kind of acclaim, but most wouldn't turn their backs on it and, in fact, most covet it. Whether it's because fame means better parts and more control over one's career or simply because it gives personal pleasure, most actors are more than willing to put up with the negative side of public acclaim if they could just get a taste of it. Every actor feels that he or she has a special quality—and the desire and perhaps the need to exhibit it. Acting is about reaching out and touching people, moving people, making people attend to you. If numbers mean anything, then stardom affords the ultimate satisfaction—the chance to communicate one's art to hundreds of thousands. Can you plan to be a star? Can you guide yourself up into the top of the top? How can you become one of the chosen? I don't know, and I don't think anyone in the profession can give you an honest answer. The acting business is an unpredictable and fickle and unfaithful love and no one can forecast how it will treat you. Some actors believe that anyone with a very special talent will make it, no matter what. Perhaps that's so—with two qualifications: special talent plus unrelenting drive and, most important, a nearly desperate desire. If acting is and remains important enough to you, you can have yourself a career.

Index